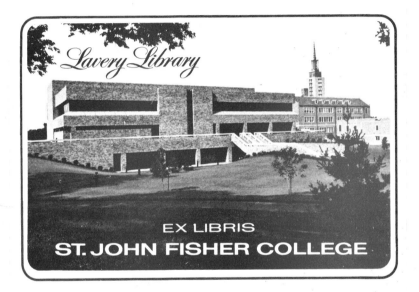

MBAs ON THE FAST TRACK

MBAs ON THE FAST TRACK
The Career Mobility of Young Managers

PHYLLIS A. WALLACE

BALLINGER PUBLISHING COMPANY
A Subsidiary of Harper & Row, Publishers, Inc.

International Standard Book Number: 0-88730-120-7

Library of Congress Catalog Card Number: 88-34180

Printed in the United States of America

Library of Congress Cataloging-in-Publication Data

Wallace, Phyllis Ann.
    MBAs on the fast track : the career mobility of young managers /
Phyllis A. Wallace.
        p. cm.
    Bibliography: p.
    Includes index.
    ISBN 0-88730-120-7
    1. Executives—United States—Promotions. 2. Career
development—United States. 3. Sloan School of
Management—Alumni. I. Title.
HD38.25.U6W35 1989
331.7′616584′00973—dc19   88-34180
                                                                  CIP

89 90 91 92 HC 10 9 8 7 6 5 4 3 2 1

To Master of Science in Management Graduates
of the Sloan School of Management at MIT
Classes of 1975–79

CONTENTS

LIST OF FIGURES

LIST OF TABLES

PREFACE

A ten-year data collection effort on the work and non-work activities of 380 Sloan Master of Science in Management graduates provides the information for this book on the career mobility of young managers. Some readers of the chapters wanted statistical documentation for nearly every statement while others recommended that I relegate the numbers to the appendices. I have tried to strike a balanced approach using statistics in support of significant or controversial issues and case studies to tell the stories of different individuals. Another source of tension in the presentation of data has been in the different perspectives of economists and social psychologists in viewing labor market activities. Although I have been inclined to emphasize the more narrow focus of salaries as success indicators, I have included as many of the more qualitative and difficult-to-measure variables as possible.

The primary reason for initiating the study was to compare economic outcomes between men and women over a five-year period. Soon it became apparent that although their numbers were fewer, the minority Sloan MBAs were not doing as well as their Sloan peers. Thus, a separate chapter on the minority experience, especially that of black males, has been included. More resources would have allowed for a more extensive analysis of the data, but the outcomes would probably have been the same. Several major questions still remain on why male and female MBAs' experiences have differed, and these questions have been noted for future researchers.

ACKNOWLEDGMENTS

I am especially indebted to several organizations and a number of individuals who supported and sustained this research during the past thirteen years. Longitudinal research activities, which track the same groups of individuals over several years, are rarely choice projects for funding sponsors. The Office of the Dean, Master's Program Office, Behavioral and Policy Studies Area, and the Industrial Relations Section at the Sloan School provided continual funding for research assistance. In the early stages of the project, the General Motors Foundation and the Millipore Company were helpful. At a later crucial stage of coding and computer data entry The Stop and Shop Foundation funded that work.

Research assistance was provided at various times by these Sloan School students: Maryellen Kelley, Cynthia Palmer, Paul Cournoyer, and Michael Even. Major statistical analysis was performed by Ming-Je Tang, and the long-term research assistance of Cathleen Tilney improved the final product. Over the years, secretarial support was given by Joyce Yearwood who typed the questionnaires and transcriptions of interviews. Deborah Hannon typed the early drafts of the manuscript, and Graham Ramsay was especially efficient in producing the numerous versions of the final draft. Since this book includes a large number of lengthy statistical tables, I wish to thank the support staff for their contributions. Emily Maggazu's Standard Industrial Classification (SIC) codes and list of employers of Sloan School graduates enabled me to keep up with a fairly mobile group.

Jan Austin-Scott handled some of the administrative chores of completing the final draft. Marie Deuerlein checked all of the references and molded the bibliography into a consistent format.

A number of colleagues read selected chapters, but my own assessment of substance and form has prevailed. I believe that the various drafts benefited from their thoughtful reviews. I should like to thank Bernard Anderson, Lotte Bailyn, Lisa Lynch, Allen Lee, Annette LaMond, Julianne Malveaux, Charles Myers, Robert McKersie, Paul Osterman, Josephine Olson, Edgar Schein, and Lester Thurow. Charles Myers also encouraged me not to abandon the project after several years of work and at a time when I was trying to cope with a personal tragedy.

Throughout these past thirteen years I have enjoyed my discussions with Sloan School graduates. Occasionally I have met their parents, spouses, and received photographs of their offspring—the Sloans of the next century. To all of the individuals listed above, but especially to the Sloan School graduates of the Classes of 1975–79 who participated over a five-year period, I am grateful.

1 INTRODUCTION

In 1986, just under 10 percent of the employed persons in the United States were in executive, administrative, and managerial positions. Although this ratio has been sustained over the past two decades, less than 70 percent of the 10.6 million persons in this category in 1986 represented a more narrowly defined managerial group. This book focuses on the MBA (Master of Business Administration) component of the managerial population. Master's degrees conferred in business and management increased fourfold from 17,868 in 1968 to 70,000 in 1986. It is from this highly educated and talented pool, now well represented in entry level and middle management positions, that the CEOs (chief executive officers) of the next few decades will be selected. Only about 17 percent of the top CEOs today have MBAs.

Management as a practical occupation is relatively new. With the separation of ownership and management stemming from the Industrial Revolution, individuals were needed who would manage assets that they did not own and whose performance would be measured based on the output of others. These hired managers now operate in a variety of organizations, in different functions, and at different levels of authority. In the initial stages of their careers in management, individuals work in specialized roles, such as financial analysis, in which they undertake specified tasks but do not manage people.

Later they may serve as team leaders, rotating from project to project, which is the norm for management consulting and the merger and acquisitions activities in investment banking.

Another significant career stage may occur when individuals become general managers, who not only integrate across functions but have major responsibility for others. These managers plan and monitor operations, resolve conflicts, and—at the most senior levels—wield the kind of power that helps to shape the direction of the organization. They deal with the major clients of the organization—the shareholders, employees, customers, trade associations, as well as the larger community. For example, a major commercial bank's decision to allocate resources to an educational program for inner city youth would indicate that the CEO considers this an appropriate item in the organization's strategic plan.

The American managerial work force is being transformed by shifts from a manufacturing to a service-based economy, the widespread use of personal computers, enhanced communications capabilities, the globalization of markets, the turbulence in the regulatory environment, and the increased heterogeneity of the labor force. Managers will now have to function in a more complex and interdependent environment. MBAs have been trained to solve problems, and their on-the-job experiences will teach them to do so in settings of uncertainty, ambiguity, and time pressures.

THE STUDY

In this study of the career movements of young managers (average age at graduation of twenty-seven years), the data collected from 321 graduates of the Sloan School of Management at the Massachusetts Institute of Technology (MIT) was analyzed. Although the degree granted by the Sloan School is technically a Master of Science in management, it is considered comparable to the Master in Business Administration (MBA) awarded by most business schools. Throughout this text the graduates of the Sloan School are referred to as Sloan MBAs. Individuals from five graduating classes of 1975 through 1979 were surveyed at four points during the first five years of their post-management school careers. (See Figure 1-1.)

Five years seemed long enough for individuals to become established in the upper ranks of middle management. The purpose of the

Figure 1-1. Data Collection on Sloan MBAs by Years.

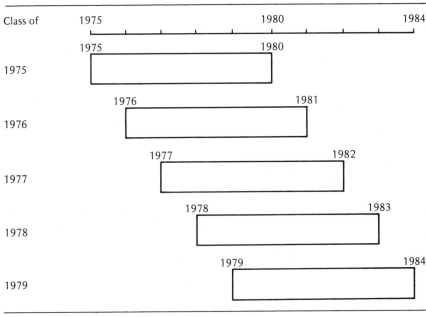

See Table 1-1.

study was to document the job changes, promotions, salary increases, performance appraisals, problems, and concerns, as they occurred in their professional lives. Sloan MBAs received questionnaires shortly before they were graduated and were surveyed one, two, and five years later. Tracking the Sloan MBAs encompassed ten years of data collection activity (1975-84).

Although several women per year had graduated from the Master's Program of the Sloan School during the 1960s and early 1970s, 1975 was the first year in which women accounted for a significant percentage of the graduates. Sixteen women represented 12 percent of that graduating class, and by 1979 women represented 25 percent of the graduating class. At the end of the academic year 1974-75 only 3,063 women received MBAs from institutions of higher education in the United States. They represented 8.4 percent of all MBAs granted that year, but were more than quadruple the 749 women MBAs who had been graduated five years earlier.

Women MBAs were becoming an increasing proportion of the MBA pool, but in the middle 1970s there was considerable debate about whether equally qualified women who pursued managerial careers would achieve as much as their male peers. The prevailing conventional wisdom was that many would find these non-traditional jobs extraordinarily difficult, and would shift to less demanding positions. Or, it was assumed that for those women who remained in the male-dominated managerial jobs, their progress would lag behind their male peers. It was also thought that the attrition rate would be high as young women sought to mesh work and their personal lives, especially families and children. Determining whether women MBAs would have the same commitment to their careers as comparable males could be documented and assessed through a long-term tracking of individuals as their careers evolved. Thus, in May 1975, one month before the class of 1975 graduation, a decision was made to undertake such research. A brief questionnaire was designed, and women graduates and their male peers were asked whether they would participate in a five-year effort to assess their post-graduation career progress.

Two groups were excluded from the sample of Sloan MBAs. Foreign students, in some years representing nearly one-fifth of the class, were not included. However, Sloan MBAs who were U.S. citizens and assigned to overseas posts were included; these sent in their responses from Japan, Indonesia, Saudi Arabia, London, and Ireland. Sloan Fellows, who also receive the same Master of Science degree in management as students in the regular two-year Master's Program, were in a special twelve-month executive development program and were also excluded. The Fellows were older, more experienced, and usually sponsored by their employers as likely candidates to move into senior management. During 1975–79 approximately 534 individuals (excluding these two groups) were graduated from the Master's Program at the Sloan School. The initial sample of 321 individuals (113 women and 208 men) was supplemented by 52 males from the classes of 1975 and 1976 for whom information is available only for the initial and five-year surveys.[1] Thus, approximately two-thirds of all Sloan MBAs for the 1975–79 period are in the surveys. Several individuals who received the degree in September or January rather than in June may have been missed.

The one-year, follow-up surveys were not coded or entered into the computerized data set for statistical analysis, but they were carefully scrutinized, and used as background materials. These surveys focused on the Sloan graduates' transition to full-time work from full-time student status. At least one-third of the students had entered the graduate program directly from undergraduate school and had no full-time work experience. Others, particularly women, had previously worked in the public sector or in nonprofit organizations and had to adjust to private sector employment procedures and different expectations. Also, in the first three years of the study, a sizeable number of men enrolled in the graduate management program after completing military service. Their post-Sloan School careers represented a transition to civilian jobs.

The initial questionnaire (See Appendix B) asked the graduates about their undergraduate majors, prior work experience, functional concentration while at the Sloan School, job title, salary, the name of their employer for their initial post-graduation job, and some selected demographic information. Thirty-five percent of the Sloan graduates were women and slightly more than 7 percent were minorities. One-third of the survey participants had undergraduate majors in engineering, mathematics, and science, while almost two-fifths of them had selected finance as their area of concentration in management school.

The primary objective of the longitudinal study was to determine whether women and men who had received similar job offers upon graduation had reached comparable levels in middle management five years later, and also received equivalent pay. Detailed information on the industry of employment, salary changes, promotions, changes in jobs, hours of work, work-related travel, performance appraisals, supervisory responsibilities, job satisfaction, productivity relative to peers, career path changes, and significant lifestyle changes were collected in the two-year surveys. (See Appendix B for two-year, follow-up questionnaires.) The analysis provides a snapshot of the status of Sloan MBAs two years into their careers and identifies variables that are good predictors for status at the end of the fifth year. The lengthier five-year surveys, in addition, covered the individual's level in the organization, relations with peers, supervisors and mentors, job-related stress, dual career marriages, children, and non-work related activities. (See Appendix B.) A data set including all of the above activities for each Sloan MBA over a five-year period was established.

The aggregate response rate was 78 percent for the two-year survey and 68 percent for the five-year follow-up survey. (See Table 1-1.) A major effort was made to encourage response. Individuals had the option of providing written responses to the questionnaires or being interviewed by telephone at their convenience. Two invest-

Table 1-1. Sloan School Respondents, Classes of 1975–79.[a]

| | Initial Survey | | |
Class	Total	Women	Men
1975	34	16	18
1976	42	19	23
1977	87	27	60
1978	74	23	51
1979	84	28	56
Total	321	113	208
	Two-Year Survey		
1975	32	14	18
1976	41	20	21
1977	66	19	47
1978	55	15	40
1979	57	19	38
Total	251	87	164
	Five-Year Survey		
1975	29	13	16
1976	35	18	17
1977	57	18	39
1978	49	16	33
1979	49	19	30
Total	219	84	135

a. A few respondents were full-time students, temporarily unemployed or not in the labor force.

ment bankers who were working eighty-hour weeks scheduled tele-phone interviews at home on Sunday morning. Some of the MBAs who worked in the greater Boston area scheduled face-to-face inter-views at the Sloan School. During the ten-year data collection period, several factors may have encouraged a high response rate. All partici-pants were notified with the initial survey that a summary profile of their class would be prepared after the second year and fifth year sur-veys, and these preliminary reports were sent to the respondents.

Sloan MBAs continued to compare their achievements with members of their Sloan class even as they competed with their peers at work. At the two-year survey, they overwhelmingly considered themselves to be more productive and perhaps superior to their peers at work. Also, during the data collection period, the Sloan School restructured the Master's Program core curriculum; respondents to the five-year surveys were asked to assess the strengths and weaknesses of their management education and to suggest changes. Even before this exercise, the respondents had been informed that as a result of their identification of deficiencies in communication skills (in a response to a query on the second year survey), the Sloan School had established writing workshops and was considering including attendance at a communications workshop as part of the core requirement. For these reasons, response rates were fairly high for a group in which some individuals had relocated several times or lived overseas during the five-year period. Follow-up letters and/or telephone calls were made to encourage response by all graduates, but because the minority subsample was relatively small, more additional follow-up (telephone calls and letters) were used for these graduates.

Thirty-six individuals who responded to the various questionnaires were excluded, because they were full-time students, temporarily unemployed, or out of the labor market. Nine Sloan MBAs enrolled in Ph.D. programs or law schools. Eight individuals were temporarily unemployed. The reason for temporary unemployment varied over the five-year period. Initially, the unemployed were men who conducted a job search several months after graduation. Later, the unemployed were women who had relocated with their spouses and were seeking jobs comparable to their prior positions. Three individuals were out of the labor market due to health reasons. Also by the fifth year, nine women were part-time employees because they were taking care of small children. Finally, seven other individuals had elected to pursue careers in non-business-related fields. The tables presented in this book, unless otherwise specified, show only full-time, employed Sloan MBAs.

Since compensation (salary plus bonuses and fringe benefits) is widely accepted by labor market specialists as the best measure of upward mobility and success, a separate chapter is devoted to these issues. A comparison is made between the scholarly literature on MBA compensation and the study's findings that Sloan women MBAs, five years after graduation, have received the same pay as their male peers from management school. Sloan graduates reported high levels of career success, personal success, and above-average job satisfaction. Although Sloan women earned the same level of salary after five years, their psychic costs were higher. The level of reported stress was significantly higher for women, and at the time of the two-year surveys women also reported longer work hours per week. Thus, women MBAs endured greater hardships in order to attain the same compensation and rewards as their male counterparts.

The chapters in this book examine the early careers of the Sloan MBAs within the larger context of the managerial challenges of the future. Throughout the study the primary comparisons are between female and male managers. Chapter 2 reviews the status of women managers during the past two decades. Chapter 3 profiles the Sloan MBAs at the time of the initial, two-year, and five-year surveys. Chapter 4 discusses one of the most significant variables of the study, industry of employment, and traces the migrations into and out of key industries over the five years. An interesting outcome here was that even though almost one-quarter of the graduates accepted jobs initially in management consulting, by the fifth year, manufacturing including high technology was the major industry of employment. Chapter 5 is devoted to compensation, for it is in this area that there is considerable debate about the achievements of women managers.

In Chapter 6 the status of minority managers is examined, especially blacks in the private sector and how well the minority Sloan MBAs have done compared to their Sloan peers is assessed. For a number of reasons, the minority Sloan MBAs who were graduated between 1975 and 1979 lagged significantly behind their Sloan counterparts' career success five years after graduation. Chapter 7 summarizes and proposes a response to the basic question of what lessons were learned from the perspectives of MBAs and managers, the management education organizations, and the American economy. Chapters 3 through 5 include numerous statistical tables. One major table on the shifts over time among the industries of employment is included in Appendix A, since it appropriately documents the findings in several chapters. An extensive bibliography that includes texts on women in management and minorities in management has been compiled.

One of the Sloan MBAs urged the author not to restrict the analysis to statistical presentations but also to use some case studies so that readers would know that "real people" were involved. Chapter 4 presents a series of case studies of women MBAs in management consulting. Management consulting was the new growth industry of the 1970s and women were newcomers to this industry. Almost one-quarter of the Sloan MBAs started their post-management school careers in management consulting. Case studies are used again in the chapter on minority MBAs both because the sample is too small for use of refined statistical techniques and because the respondents have discussed their experiences in the private sector at some length.

The subtitle of this book is "Career Mobility of Young Managers." These occupational careers are viewed mainly from an external perspective of industry of employment, job level, salary, and tasks. What John Van Maanen has termed the internal perspective of careers—"aspirations, expectations, evaluations, and role conflicts arising from work/nonwork demands"—has been a secondary concern.[2]

Whether the Sloan MBAs were the forerunners of the types of managers needed for the next decade is still an open question. Certainly, their representative job descriptions at year five, shown below, would indicate that they are well positioned to be the managers of the future.

Selected Job Descriptions of Sloan MBAs at Year Five:

1. *Manager of Decision Support Systems*—Design, develop, and implement computerized financial and product planning systems.

2. *Director of Product Marketing*—Manage group concerned with definition and coordination of new products and provide technical support for existing products.

3. *Manager of Technical Volume Forecasting and Business Planning*—Translate perceived customer demand and marketing strategies into financial commitment and material shipment plans, committing 25 percent of the manufacturing base and $300 million of materials.

4. *Director of Employee Relations*—Responsible for all employee relations at six large facilities including employment, human resources, salary administration, and other personnel activity.

5. *Director of Strategic Planning-Domestic Manufacturing*—Responsible for implementing formal strategic planning process and assisting management in the evolution of plans, development of priorities, allocation of resources, and tracking of performance.

6. *Manager of Manufacturing Support*—Manage group of eighteen software engineers performing all facets of external product development.

NOTES

1. It should be noted that in 1975 and 1976, all female, but only a sample of the male, graduates were given questionnaires. This methodology of matching a female Sloan graduate with a comparable male was not used after 1976. In 1982, surveys were sent to men who had been excluded in 1975 and 1976, and fifty-two of them responded with first and fifth year information. This group is referred to as "Short Five" respondents. The profile of the Short Fives was similar to that of the selected male respondents from 1975 and 1976 with two minor exceptions. There were slightly more engineers in the Short Five group, and a higher proportion had concentrated in finance while attending Sloan School. As will be shown in Chapter 5, neither undergraduate major nor area of concentration were significant variables in determining compensation in the fifth year. Achievements of each sample over the five-year period were comparable.
2. John Van Maanen, "Summary: Towards a Theory of the Career," in J. Van Maanen, ed., *Organizational Careers: Some Perspectives* (New York: John Wiley and Sons, 1977), ch. 8, pp. 167–68.

2 WOMEN MANAGERS
A Review of the Literature

Since women MBAs are compared to their male counterparts in this book, we begin with a review of the status of women managers during the past two decades. These findings provide the context for the longitudinal study of graduates from the Master's Program in Management at the Sloan School at MIT. The primary objective of the study was to determine whether female and male graduates—who had received comparable job offers upon graduation from business school—reached comparable levels in middle management five years later and also received equivalent pay. The research literature on women in management has thus far yielded competing hypotheses on the status of women managers.

Dipboye's critical review of organizational behavior research notes several studies, indicating that women who are highly educated, work in traditionally male work settings, and are at higher levels of management appear to conform more to the stereotype of the successful manager and less to the traditional female stereotype.[1] Another body of research from the economic literature focuses on the persistence of salary differentials between women and men managers. These empirical studies offer competing explanations of economic success based on either productivity differences or labor market discrimination.[2]

The recent research and numerous articles in business publications note that success in management for women has been difficult as

11

they have aspired to senior positions. Although women managers at entry level and middle management positions may have overcome many hurdles, they appear to have to confront more barriers than their male peers as they compete for the top jobs. Notwithstanding significant shifts in societal perspectives, implementation of anti-discrimination laws, and expanding opportunities for managerial jobs, women continue to have greater difficulty moving into upper management positions. Research here focuses on women managers now ready for upward mobility.

The number of women managers (in official U.S. Department of Labor categories of executive, administrative, and management positions) more than tripled during the past twenty years. But in 1986 they accounted for only 37 percent of this broad occupational category, up from 15 percent in 1966. There were about 1 million women employed as managers in 1966 and 3.9 million, or about 9 percent of the total female labor force, in 1986.[3] The total managerial work force from both the public and private sectors represented one-tenth of all employed workers. The women's share of private sector managerial jobs, as reported in annual surveys of the Equal Employment Opportunity Commission (EEOC), the agency responsible for implementation of employment anti-discrimination laws, had increased from 9 percent in 1966 to 23 percent in 1984.[4] During the 1970s there was an explosive growth in the number of highly educated individuals who entered management by way of a graduate degree, usually the master in management/business administration (MBA). Approximately 70,000 MBAs were granted in 1986 as compared with 21,000 granted in 1970. Women MBAs had increased from 4 percent of the total in 1972 to about one-third in 1986.[5]

During the past twenty years, changing attitudes about women in non-traditional jobs, implementation of anti-discrimination legislation, and the outstanding performance of the first women pioneers in the field helped to expand opportunities for women in management. Women are now well represented in middle management—but will a significant number of these young, better educated, and achievement-oriented women attain influential senior management positions within the next decade? Whether career success is gauged by compensation or some other proxy of labor market outcomes, conventional wisdom suggests that advancement for women into senior management may not be as easy as was anticipated a decade ago.

In June 1987, *Business Week* identified fifty of the highest-ranked female executives who were "within striking distance" of becoming CEOs. But in the same cover story, the publication reviewed the status of some of the 100 leading corporate women included in a similar survey in 1976, and found that nearly one-third had left their corporate jobs because they had hit the "glass ceiling" or, if still working, were pigeonholed in staff jobs.[6] Women managers had moved from entry level positions to a solid presence in middle management, but the breakthrough to the upper echelons of management appeared to be "opting out," "topping out," or "throttling back on their ambitions." Two former practitioners who are now observers of women in corporations ask rhetorically whether a critical mass of extraordinarily well-trained but "burned out" cases are about to collect on the doorstep of corporate America.[7]

The rise of women into the ranks of middle management could not have occurred without dramatic changes in attitudes by their supervisors, male peers, subordinates, and society at large. The same survey of attitudes held by successful executives on women in management was conducted in 1965 and again in 1985. The results, reported in the *Harvard Business Review* (HBR), found greater acceptance of women in executive positions twenty years later.[8] In the earlier survey, only 35 percent of the male executives held favorable views of women in management as compared with 82 percent of the responding female executives. Both male and female respondents agreed that women had to be exceptionally or overly qualified in order to succeed in management. By 1985 a significant shift had occurred in the attitudes of male executives towards women managers.

The percentage of men expressing unfavorable attitudes towards women executives fell from 41 percent in 1965 to 5 percent in 1985. Although many of their negative perceptions had changed, much resistance to women managers remained, with most of the respondents still believing that women had to be exceptional to succeed in business.[9] Almost half of the women surveyed believed that women would never be completely accepted as executives in corporations. These views of corporate decisionmakers may shape the outcome of women in management, certainly for the next decade or more.

Implementation of equal employment opportunity laws have altered behavior in the workplace and eventually modified some attitudes. Title VII of the Civil Rights Act of 1964 (as amended) prohibited discrimination by employers, employment agencies, and labor unions on the basis of race, color, religion, sex, and national origin. Discrimination was proscribed in all aspects of the employment process—recruitment, hiring, discharge, compensation, training, promotion, and terms and conditions or privileges of employment.[10] Initially, white collar employees did not perceive these laws as a useful mechanism to improve their labor market status. In fact, in the 1965 survey reported in the *Harvard Business Review*, 71 percent of the men and 55 percent of the women rejected the suggestion that the law against sex discrimination would improve the status of women. By 1985, however, only 16 percent of the men and 26 percent of the women believed that this legislation had no impact on equal opportunity for women.[11]

The consent decree signed in January 1973 between the twenty-three operating companies of American Telephone and Telegraph (AT&T) and the federal agencies responsible for administration of employment discrimination laws was the first attempt to deal with sex discrimination on a comprehensive basis. The company, which at that time was the largest private employer in the United States, agreed to restructure its internal labor market over a six-year period. Goals and intermediate targets were set for a variety of occupations in the establishments of each of the operating companies.[12] By January 1979 when the decree ended, the number of women who had reached middle management and higher levels had quadrupled (from 338 to 1,374), and women accounted for 59 percent of the increase in all managerial jobs.[13] The significant improvement in the utilization of women and the sophisticated techniques developed to track human resources served as a model for later attempts by other employers to expand opportunities for women.

Expansion of employment opportunities for women workers did not, however, produce equal wages. Male and female executives in the *HBR* surveys of 1965 and 1985 disagreed on the extent of pay inequity. In 1965, 84 percent of the women and 53 percent of the men agreed with the statement, "A woman executive is invariably paid less than her male counterpart." Twenty years later the gap was still wide, with 73 percent of the women and 34 percent of the men agreeing with this statement.[14] In 1987 the median earnings of women in full-time, year-round executive, administrative, and managerial jobs were 64 percent of the men's earnings.

There is a considerable debate among economists over how much of the sustained wage differential is attributable to productivity characteristics and how much to sex discrimination. A number of empirical studies use multivariate regression analysis to decompose the male-female earnings gap by controlling for variables such as age, hours of work, marital status, work experience, continuity of work experience, education, turnover, and geographic region. In three-fourths of the studies, the variables that might affect productivity explain less than one-half of the earnings differential.[15] Some researchers have attributed much of the unexplained residual to wage discrimination.

The earnings gap between men and women in the narrowly defined managerial occupations is smaller than the aggregate earnings ratios mainly because management is a predominately male occupation with higher paying jobs. The striking sex differentials in earnings derive from the concentration of women in sex-segregated jobs. This type of occupational segregation by sex diminished in management as more young women started their careers in this area. Beller's calculations show that occupational segregation of the sexes declined continuously during the 1970s.[16] However, intra-occupational segregation in management remained high, as witnessed by the scarcity of women in senior management. In June 1987 a *Forbes* cover story on the leading players in corporate America focused on 797 powerful men and 3 powerful women. These individuals wielded great corporate power and each headed a large, publicly owned corporation.[17]

Blau and Ferber's review of the economic literature on the earnings gap would seem to indicate that younger women are likely to retain a substantial amount of the improvement in their relative earnings as they age. In 1983, women's earnings as a percent of the median income of men (working year round, full time) was 73.3 percent for the 25–34 age group, the prime working years, and 56.2 percent for the 45–54 age group. More importantly, women's income improved over time. The gains were most pronounced for the 25–34 age group whose relative income increased by almost 11 percent between 1973 and 1983 (from 62.6 percent to 73.3 percent).[18] These younger women are spending more time in the labor market and are likely to continue to fare better than their predecessors at each point of the life cycle. As this occurs, the overall sex gap in earnings should continue to decline, as the earlier cohorts of women with relatively low earnings are replaced increasingly by the more recent cohorts with higher earnings.[19] The earnings of women MBAs, nearly all recent and young entrants to management, are presently more than 80 percent of male earnings.

Higher educational attainment, intense commitment to work, sheer competence, and assimilation of traits of successful male managers (achievement of high salary, authority and responsibility, and recognition) have strengthened the position of women in management. Economists would argue that relative human capital endowments accounted for some of the improvement and that sex differences in lifetime investment in human capital are being narrowed. Human capital includes, most prominently, education, training, and innate abilities (endowments). What types of women have opted to be managers, and what is the typical profile of women in middle management and on the executive level? In 1984 *The Wall Street Journal*, with the assistance of the Gallup Organization, surveyed 722 women executives who held the title of vice president or higher in listed companies with annual sales of at least $100 million. These women managers were divided into six groups on the basis of age, salary, years of management experience, and age of entry into management. For comparisons with our research, we have examined the profiles of two groups, the "young achievers" and "top management."[20]

The young achievers (16 percent of the total sample) were under 40 years of age and had less than fifteen years of management experience. Their annual salaries averaged $60,000 or more, with 35 percent earning $100,000 or more. Fifty-five percent of the group had attended graduate school and one in four had an MBA. About half of the group was married (a proportion that was significantly less than the national norms for women) and close to two-thirds had no children. These young achievers were 'fast trackers' in general management, finance, sales, and marketing.[21] Senior women managers or executive women have been defined in a variety of ways by researchers. They are usually an older group with more than fifteen years of management experience. Many started their careers as secretaries or in other non-managerial positions. Having reached the upper levels of middle management or the bottom of senior management, most of these women do not expect to become CEOs, or even company presidents. Korn/Fery International in collaboration with the Graduate School of Management at UCLA conducted a 1982 survey of women senior executives from large U.S. companies. Their study revealed a similar profile of a forty-six-year-old white Protestant woman who was not currently married and had no children. Most had attained the rank of vice president or higher and earned an annual compensation of $92,159, as contrasted to $116,000 earned by senior level male executives from Fortune 500 companies. The same number, 34 percent of the women executives, began their careers in managerial capacities as in clerical and secretarial positions.[22]

The Wall Street Journal survey categorized its top management women, 15 percent of the total sample, as mostly over forty years of age with a minimum of fifteen years of management experience and annual salaries of $75,000 or more. Less than half were married and a majority had no children. Like the young achievers, the top management women devoted long hours (a sixty-hour work week for many) to their careers. These pioneering women have had to deal with traditional sex-role attitudes as they have earned the respect of male peers, subordinates, and supervisors. Still, four out of five of the total sample of women executives said that there were disadvantages to being female in the business world and 70 percent felt that they were paid less than a man of equal ability.[23]

The Wall Street Journal headline on one of its articles based on the survey read "Young Executive Women Advance Farther, Faster Than Predecessors," and indicated that the younger women entered the corporation as managers, compared to many older women who were promoted into management from the secretarial ranks. In their study of the career development of successful personnel, Larwood and Gattiker found that older and younger women had substantially the same level of success and attained similar situations at the same time, whereas younger men appear to lag behind older men.[24] Another look at senior women reveals that women managers who have been trailblazers in a male-dominated environment still perceive major problems of unequal opportunity, male resistance, and numerous barriers.

One group of twenty senior women from a large manufacturing firm shared their views with the author. All were near the top of the corporate hierarchy, having reached levels close to the CEO. The average age was forty-one years, and most were single or divorced. The married women, all part of dual career couples, had children. Most of the senior women had graduate degrees, with a few Ph.D.s and some MBAs. They had risen to top levels of the company through the manufacturing, engineering, and marketing functions, and currently averaged a forty-eight hour work week. While these senior women have been successful, as measured by their corporate level, and felt that they could grow and be challenged within the company, they were unanimous in expressing their concern that good representation of women at the top of the corporate hierarchy would not occur for another decade, if at all.

Their responses to one of the survey questions: *How soon do you see a good representation of women in top management? What might facilitate this process?* reveal considerable pessimism. For example: "I do not see a good representation at any of the levels above me and really don't see how this will change given the corporate culture and the politics women would have to buy into." "Never, changing the culture so that it values (not only tolerates) different leadership styles." "Representation is getting better but it may level off now that the hidden wall has been moved." Written responses indicated that the hidden wall was once perceived to be at a lower level but once these senior women had broken through the wall was moved up several levels. These women had learned to 'work' the system. They had established networks and had identified short-term mentors, enabling them to participate in the highly mobile company culture. They were aware of the need to solicit information and were not hampered by set channels for all interactions. These women were in contact with the CEO and senior officials as well as their peers and their subordinates. Their pessimism regarding improved representation of women in the top levels of the company is surprising, given their own successes. However, some research indicates that women managers tend to see themselves as performing more poorly than their male peers.[25] Some of the women's pessimism may be due to the attitudes of male senior managers and some to their own need for a more balanced professional-personal life. One respondent noted that a far more difficult achievement than her climb up the corporate ladder was her survival of a twenty-year marriage with a dual career partner.

Finally, a 1986 survey by Heidrick and Struggles found that the typical corporate woman officer was a forty-four-year old white Protestant employed at the vice presidential level or above by a $2 billion plus non-industrial organization. These women earned a cash compensation of $115,810 with those in the 40–49 age group receiving the highest pay. Almost one in ten from this age group was in the $250,000 or above salary category. As in the other surveys of senior women executives, a lower percentage (58 percent) were married than is typical either of the national norm for women or for male senior level executives. Most of these women did not have children. In an interesting comparison of a similar survey conducted by the same organization in 1980, fewer of the senior women six years later had started their careers in clerical positions and more than half held advanced degrees. These women have ranked hard work, intelligence, and leadership as the top criteria contributing to their professional success.[26]

However, the transition from middle manager to senior level executive is not an easy one. Apparently, hundreds of the brightest women managers are leaving corporations for smaller companies. Is their progress blocked beyond middle management? Why have management opportunities in the upper echelons fallen short of expectations? In August 1986 *Fortune*, reporting on why women managers were bailing out, analyzed the career paths of men and women who had received MBAs in 1976 from seventeen of the most selective business schools. Thirty percent of 1,039 women reported on their alumni/ae questionnaires that they were either self-employed or unemployed, or listed no occupation. By comparison, 21 percent of the 4,255 men listed either self-employment or no occupation.[27]

The research literature has produced different ways of viewing the topping out of corporate women. This period of adult adjustment has been described by career theorists as mid-crisis (age 35–45) as a major reassessment of one's progress relative to one's ambitions, forcing decisions to level off, change careers, or forge ahead to new and higher challenges.[28]

Assessing one's dreams and hopes against realities is a part of the mid-life transition. For many individuals, there is a period of crisis during which a major reassessment must be made of how one is doing relative to one's ambitions and the importance of work and/or career to one's total life experience.[29]

Organizational theorists who recently and critically examined this classic model of career development have labelled it as one typical of careers traditionally expected of successful males. Larwood and Gattiker have proposed an alternative model which suggests that the careers of women are substantially different from those of men, and that this requires a consideration not only of family and competing demands external to the work environment but of phenomena that may distinguish between men and women. They believe that a broad model of women's career development may improve our knowledge of the non-conforming man. In their schema, they also include an alternative neoclassical model of organizational development in which theorists agree that competing family demands and individual preferences interact with organizational needs to affect careers of both men and women.[30]

Numerous questions remain. If women managers are merely experiencing the mid-career assessment that their male counterparts face, then why is there such an outcry about glass ceilings and "success and betrayal?" In caustic terms, Hardesty and Jacobs wrote of women managers' success and corporate betrayal. They assert that the corporate disillusionment that women are now experiencing is largely different from doubts corporate men have traditionally confronted. They believe that women bring a second, private agenda to the corporate experiences—an agenda of which men are largely unaware: "Today's corporate woman torn between expectations of success and the reality of continued limitations is the product of an independent combination of historical forces, media hype, and the myths and expectations with which they were raised."[31]

If women managers are not reaching the top positions, is it because they are still devoting considerable time to their families? What about the single women? In all of the surveys noted above single women executives account for a third or more of the total sample. They do not appear to have achieved more than women executives who are married—or, is managerial achievement radical and deviant behavior for all women?[32] At the lower levels of management, both men and women resemble each other psychologically, according to Harlan and Weiss, and perform effectively as managers. As they advance up the corporate hierarchy, however, women face strong sex bias (stereotypic attitudes, greater pressures to perform exceptionally well, and exclusion from some settings), which limits how far they can move into senior management.[33]

There is no consensus in the research on what constitutes the primary reasons for limited upward mobility of women in management. Kanter has hypothesized that productivity, motivation, and career success is determined by the structure of organizations and the nature of social circumstances: "Thus, observed differences in the behavior and the success of women and men had more to do with what they were handed by the organization than with inherent differences in ability or drive."[34] Harlan and Weiss contend that the interaction of both individual traits of women (early socialization experiences, risk aversion, low aspiration, role conflict and overload) and organizational structure determine managerial advancement and the exercise of power.[35] Harriman states that men come to the workplace, a primary arena for the validation of their masculinity. They form cohesive groups that exert power within the organization, and they use the power of these groups to control the culture and to exclude and isolate individuals, such as women and minority group members, who constitute a threat.[36]

These models of managerial behavior deal with the acquisition and exercise of both formal and informal power, through interaction with others. Documentation of the extent to which high-level men and women managers wield different amounts of power requires more research. We need detailed case studies of the women managers who have hit the glass ceiling. While such women may share their perspectives with individual therapists, few may be willing even in the context of anonymous research to admit that they have "failed."

The typology of most organizational theorists is based on the corporate pyramid, but numerous changes are occurring. The service economy that now typifies the United States is characterized by smaller organizations with flatter hierarchical structures. These flatter structures allocate authority to a wider base of individuals, thereby decentralizing responsibility. Many corporations have restructured and shrunk their managerial levels. Certainly, management consulting, the preferred employment of many MBAs, deviates from the corporate mold. Finally, information technology is revolutionizing the managerial landscape. Is it likely that with a less structured organization women managers will reach the most senior positions? However this scenario is scripted over the next decade, a larger pool of women managers will be there to test the system.

In the next three chapters the performance of a specific group of women MBAs is compared with that of their male peers from the Sloan School. We identify and examine significant determinants of compensation such as industry of employment, prior work experience, mentoring, hours worked per week, and travel time. We also note that constraints and facilitating factors for upward mobility in managerial careers.

NOTES

1. Robert L. Dipboye, "Problems and Progress of Women in Management," in K.S. Koziara, M.H. Moskow, and L.D. Tanner, eds., *Working Women* (Washington, D.C.: The Bureau of National Affairs, Inc., 1987), p. 124.

2. Janice F. Madden, "The Persistence of Pay Differentials," in L. Larwood, A.H. Stromberg, and B.A. Guter, eds., *Women and Work*, Vol. 1 (Beverly Hills, Calif.: Sage Publications, 1985), pp. 76-114.

3. U.S. Department of Labor, Bureau of Labor, Bureau of Labor Statistics, *Employment and Earnings* (Washington, D.C.: U.S. Government Printing Office, various years).

4. U.S. Equal Employment Opportunity Commission, *Job Patterns for Minorities and Women in Private Industry* (Washington, D.C.: U.S. Government Printing Office, various years).

5. National Center for Education Statistics, *Digest of Educational Statistics* (Washington, D.C.: U.S. Government Printing Office, various years).

6. Laurie Baum, "Corporate Women: They're About to Break Through to the Top," *Business Week*, June 22, 1987.

7. Sarah Hardesty and Nehama Jacobs, *Success and Betrayal* (New York: Franklin Watts, 1986), pp. 258-59.

8. Charlotte Decker Sutton and Kris K. More, "Executive Women—20 Years Later," *Harvard Business Review* 63 (September–October 1985): 42-66.

9. Ibid., p. 50.

10. Equal Employment Opportunity Act of 1972 (amendment to Title VII of Civil Rights Act of 1964), Public Law 92-261, March 24, 1972, 42 U.S.C. 2000e, *et seq.*

11. Sutton and More, "Executive Women," p. 52.

12. Phyllis A. Wallace, ed., *Equal Employment Opportunity and the AT&T Case* (Cambridge, Mass.: The MIT Press, 1976), pp. 269-346.

13. Phyllis A. Wallace, ed., *Women in the Workplace* (Boston: Auburn House Publishing Company, 1982), pp. 16-20.

14. Sutton and More, "Executive Women," p. 52.

15. Madden, "Persistence," pp. 83-85.

16. Andrea H. Beller, "Trends in Occupational Segregation By Sex and Race, 1960-1981," in B.F. Riskin, ed., *Sex Segregation in the Workplace* (Washington, D.C.: National Academy Press, 1984), pp. 11-26.

17. "The Boss: The 797 Most Powerful Men and 3 Most Powerful Women in Corporate America," *Forbes*, June 15, 1987.

18. Francine D. Blau and Marianne A. Ferber, "Occupations and Earnings of Women Workers," in *Working Women*, pp. 45-6.

19. Ibid.

20. "Survey of Women Executives," *The Wall Street Journal* (Dow Jones and Company, Inc., October 1984).

21. Ibid., p. 7.

22. Korn/Ferry International, "Profile of Women Senior Executives" (Los Angeles, Calif.: Korn/Ferry International, November 1982).

23. "Survey of Women Executives," p. 29.

24. Laurie Larwood and Urs. E. Gattiker, "A Comparison of the Career Paths Used By Successful Women and Men," in B. Gutek and L. Larwood, eds.,

Women's Career Development (Newbury Park, Calif.: Sage Publications, 1987), pp. 129–56.

25. Dipboye, "Problems and Progress," p. 126.

26. Heidrick and Struggles, Inc., *The Corporate Woman Officer* (Chicago: Heidrick and Struggles, 1986).

27. Alex Taylor III, "Why Women Managers Are Bailing Out," *Fortune*, August 18, 1986.

28. Edgar H. Schein, *Career Dynamics* (Reading, Mass.: Addison-Wesley Publishing Co., 1978), pp. 36–48.

29. Ibid.

30. Larwood and Gattiker, "Career Paths."

31. Hardesty and Jacobs, *Success and Betrayal*, p. 18.

32. Carolyn R. Dexter, "Women and the Exercise of Power in Organizations," in *Women and Work*, p. 245.

33. Anne Harlan and Carol L. Weiss, "Sex Differences in Factors Affecting Managerial Career Advancement," in P. Wallace, ed., *Women in the Workplace* (Boston: Auburn House Publishing Co., 1982), pp. 59–100.

34. Carole K. Barnett, "Men and Women of the Corporation Revisited: Interview with Rosabeth Moss Kanter," *Human Resource Management* 26 (Summer 1987): 257.

35. Harlan and Weiss, "Sex Differences."

36. Ann Harriman, *Women/Men/Management* (New York: Praeger Publishers, 1985), p. 137.

3 PROFILES OF SLOAN MBAs

MBAs are talented, well-educated individuals who enter management with highly specific skills and considerable motivation, ambition, and energy. They typically begin their post-graduation careers as functional experts whose primary contributions may be in consulting, portfolio management, financial analysis, or design of information systems. The first five years of their postgraduate careers, the primary focus of this book, is perceived as a period of learning, exploration, and establishing a track record. These establishment years are influential in shaping future career outcomes. Rosenbaum's tournament model of career mobility posits that assessments of an employee's first few years have profound and enduring effects on parameters of late career moves.[1] Veiga's study of mobility influences during managerial career stages concludes that time in the first position is a fairly powerful predictor of a manager's rate of career movement, not only in the early stages of a career but throughout all stages.[2]

The three surveys of Sloan MBAs discussed in this chapter indicate that for the first two years of post-management school work experience, the outcomes for both men and women were comparable. Their job assignments, career movements, productivity, and job satisfaction were not significantly different. However, between the second and the fifth year surveys some divergence emerged in male/female career patterns. Women tended to migrate to different industries, experience more job-related stress, relocate to new geographic areas at lower salaries, and 11 percent became part-time workers by year five. All of this occurred in the context of seemingly equal treatment with respect to salaries and promotions. These negative effects of career paths have been labeled the psychic costs of achievement. At the time of the fifth year survey the divergence in work experience was apparent but not of such a magnitude that it had undermined the overall achievement of women MBAs. The following sections show detailed statistical data from the surveys of the initial, second, and fifth years and highlight the comparative performance of men and women.

PROFILE OF SLOAN MBAs UPON GRADUATION, 1975-79

Table 3-1 summarizes the data collected from the initial survey of Sloan MBAs conducted for the classes of 1975 through 1979. Thirty-five percent of the sample were women and 7 percent were minorities. The average age at graduation was 27 years and more than half were single. Although almost half of the Sloan graduates had undergraduate majors in either engineering, mathematics, or the natural sciences, there were differences in the backgrounds of men and women. There were fewer women engineers, but a higher proportion of women than men had majored in mathematics and the natural sciences. Roughly a quarter of both men and women had majored in the social sciences. Economics was the social science major most selected for both men and women. Nearly two-thirds of the Sloans had full-time work experience prior to their graduate program. Nearly half of the men and about a third of the women who had prior full-time work experience were enrolled in the Accelerated Master's Program (AMP) at the Sloan School. This program enabled individuals with some work experience to complete the regular two-year Master's Program in a twelve-month period.

Although two-thirds of men and women each averaged slightly over three years of full-time work experience, men had held a richer mix of jobs. This may have enhanced their attractiveness to employers. One-fifth of the men who had worked full-time had served as military officers, some for more than five years. Another 16 percent of the men had worked a year or more as engineers, and another 10 percent had worked in such professional jobs as consultants, research scientists, product marketing managers. The Sloan women had been employed mainly in public and nonprofit jobs. They had worked as school teachers, programmers, social workers, and administrative assistants. Private employers apparently did not credit the prior work experience of many women when they sought jobs after receiving the MBA. Instead, the women may have received a slight bonus for being women, as employers sought to increase their number of female managers. Initial salaries were not significantly different for men and women, $33,350 for men and $31,910 for women (see Figure 5-1 in Chapter 5).

The leading areas for concentration for men and women while at the Sloan School were finance (38 percent of the sample), planning and control (26 percent), and MIS and operations research (15 percent). A large number of the Sloans had dual majors, and were classified into the category which they listed as their first concentration. The Sloan MBAs accepted jobs in six major industry groups—28 percent in manufacturing, 24 percent in management consulting, 20 percent in the financial services industry (including real estate, investment and commercial banking), 14 percent in high technology, and 11 percent in other services. Ninety-eight percent of all jobs were in the private sector. The "industry of employment" variable is an important determinant of fifth year success; Chapter 4 describes the industrial categories and examines retention rates for key industries. At the end of five years, women performed as well as their male Sloan School peers because they worked in the same industries. Most of the women worked in management consulting (24 percent), financial services (21 percent), and manufacturing (30 percent). The final comparison from the initial surveys shows mean beginning salaries of $31,910 for women and $33,350 for men (in constant 1983 dollars). Regardless of their prior work experience, Sloan men and women MBAs started their postgraduate management careers in the same kinds of jobs, in the same industries, and with no significant difference in salaries. Analysis of variance for initial salaries, age at graduation, and length of prior full-time work experience shows no significant differences between the men and women.

The responses on two questions from the initial survey from the first three classes differed markedly from those of the classes of 1978 and 1979. Respondents were asked where they expected to be in their careers in five years. Men answered with job titles and salary ranges. The first groups of women, however, merely indicated that

Table 3-1. Profile of Initial Survey of Sloan Master's Graduates 1975-1979[a] (*percent*).

Descriptor	*Total* *n = 321*	*Women* *n = 113*	*Men* *n = 208*
Race	100	100	100
White	93	93	92
Black and Others	7	7	8
Type of Program	100	100	100
Two-year	70	72	69
AMP	26	23	29
Five-year (SB/SM)	3	5	2
Mean Age [b]	26.7	27.4	26.7
Two-year	26.1	26.9	25.9
AMP	28.7	28.9	28.6
Five-year (SB/SM)	22.0	21.5	23.0
Marital Status	100	100	100
Single	54	57	53
Married	41	36	44
Other	4	7	3
Children	100	100	100
Have children	11	9	13
No children	87	89	85
Unknown	2	2	2
Undergraduate Major	100	100	100
Engineering	21	6	30
Mathematics	13	21	9
Social sciences	24	26	24
Natural sciences	12	14	10
Management	12	12	11
Art/Humanities	15	18	13
Other	3	3	3
Undergraduate College	100	100	100
Quality [c]	66	66	67
Other	34	34	33

Table 3-1. continued

Descriptor	Total $n = 321$	Women $n = 113$	Men $n = 208$
Sloan Concentration [d]	100	100	100
Finance	38	33	42
Organizational studies	7	7	6
MIS/Operations research	15	8	19
Market/Planning/Control	26	37	21
Applied economics	2	1	2
Industrial relations	4	6	2
International management	6	4	7
Public Systems	2	4	1
Mean Years of Prior Full-Time Work Experience	3.2	3.1	3.3
Type of Employer [e]	100	100	100
Manufacturing, (except high-tech), mining and construction	28	30	27
Management consulting	24	24	23
Finance, Insurance, Real Estate (FIRE)	8	5	10
Government/non-profit	2	4	1
Other services	11	10	12
High technology	14	11	16
Investment banking	1	2	1
Commercial banking	11	14	9
Military	1	—	1
Mean Salary [f]	32.84	31.91	33.35

a. Excludes foreign students and graduates from the Sloan Fellows Program (Executive Development).

b. 320 cases (112 females and 208 males).

c. High quality in accordance with quality rating of U.S. colleges and universities in Carnegie Commission Survey (1972). 317 cases.

d. Sloan concentration for those graduates with more than one concentration is taken as the first field mentioned on the Sloan survey. 319 cases.

e. 306 individuals. Six attended graduate or professional school on a full-time basis, and nine were either unemployed or not in the labor force and not a student.

f. 297 individuals. Salary in constant 1983 dollars (in thousands).

they expected to be working and could not be specific about position level or salary. By 1978, the women were as adept at speculating on career trajectories as the men. Respondents to the initial surveys were also asked to estimate their salaries five years after graduation. The classes of 1975 and 1976 greatly underestimated their five-year salaries, in current dollars. The actual salaries, in current dollars, started at $18,500, reached $25,700 in two years, and $46,000 in five years as compared with a projected five-year salary of $34,600. Of course, these two classes preceded the escalation in MBA salaries.

STATUS OF SLOAN MBAs AFTER TWO YEARS

The progress of Sloan MBAs two years after graduation is shown in Table 3-2, in twenty-five items from the questionnaire. Job mobility may be measured by four categories reported in the surveys: (1) changes in job titles, (2) promotions in the same company, (3) internal transfers in the same company, and (4) change of employers. Eighty percent of both men and women had changed their job titles by the second year. These changes were associated with promotions and lateral transfers with the same employers as well as change of employers, including both intra- and inter-industry shifts. The Sloan MBAs interviewed indicated that they devoted considerable effort during the first two years to finding a position with the right organizational fit for them. In Kotter's sense, they sought compatibility with their "own needs, values, strengths, and weaknesses."[3] A much larger proportion of men than women (one-third compared to one-fourth) changed employers and indicated that the primary reasons were higher compensation and better opportunities for career growth. Nearly all of these changes of employers entailed promotions or more pay. A few women relocated in order to accommodate dual career marriages, but they did not improve their compensation in the new jobs.

The larger proportion of women than men (62 percent versus 51 percent) that were promoted reflects promotion only in the same company. When internal company promotions and change of employers with significant salary increases are aggregated, more men than women had achieved promotions (79 percent as compared with 66 percent for the women). Women tended to stay with their initial employers and were promoted. Internal transfers were sometimes simultaneous with or prior to a promotion. Men had a higher propensity to change employers and to relocate geographically. Nearly all of the women changed employers for negative reasons: "changed to accommodate dual career marriage; got caught in layoff; relocated for personal reasons and was unemployed for six months; caught in the middle of a political power play; dissatisfaction with job; dissatisfaction with work, and workload; wanted more responsibility; family relocated to isolated area; position not challenging." Although men and women may have utilized different modes of movement in both the internal and external labor markets, the salary outcomes at the end of two years of $41,160 for women and $41,550 for men, were not significantly different.

Even with considerable mobility, more than two-thirds of the Sloan MBAs remained in the manufacturing, management consulting, and high technology industries. Industry of employment is discussed more fully in the next chapter, with considerable inter-industry movement within a two-year period. Although manufacturing retained fifty-five of the eighty-six individuals who were in the industry in the initial year (for a retention rate of 64 percent), twenty-three persons entered this industry from other industries by the second year. Therefore, there was a net loss of eight individuals. If the data are adjusted for non-respondents in the second year who (based on alumni records) were known to be still working in manufacturing, the retention rates are higher.

Most of the 1975–1979 Sloans classified their jobs in year two as staff jobs. Those who worked mainly as consultants were operating within an apprentice model, which at mid-point was a staff position with line responsibility. Chapter 4 describes the basic structure of the management consulting industry. While Sloan MBAs who had initially accepted positions in management consulting and the financial services industry had specific job titles, many in manufacturing and high technology discovered what the job entailed only after they had started to work. It was not until the second year follow-up survey that the study instrument asked for job descriptions as well as job titles. Even at that point, some titles seemed to be ambiguous, perhaps by choice. One woman in a large manufacturing company who was on the fast track at her company reported:

I do not have the same job as when I started two years ago. Officially my move is classified as a promotion with a geographical transfer from corporate headquarters to an operating division location. This occurred eleven months

Table 3-2. Two-Year Status, Sloan MBAs.

Descriptor	Women	% of Women Respondents[a]	Men	% of Men Respondents[a]
Total	87	100	164	100
1. Job title changes (yes)	66	80	123	81
2. Promotions, same company				
One or more	53	62	77	51
3. Internal transfer	14	16	36	23
4. Changed employers	21	25	52	33
5. Industry	85	100	158	100
Manufacturing	22	26	55	36
High tech	11	13	27	17
FIRE	5	6	10	6
Management consulting	23	27	33	21
Public	5	6	10	6
Other services	10	12	11	7
Investment banking	2	2	2	1
Commercial banking	7	8	10	6
6. Type of position in firm	85	100	158	100
Staff	33	39	76	48
Line	17	20	41	26
Staff/line	8	9	11	7
Consultant	21	25	27	17
Other	6	7	3	2

7. Hours/week	52.2	—	50.8	—
8. Mean wages (constant dollar)	$41,160	—	$41,550	—
9. Geographic Relocation (yes)	24	28	59	37
10. Internal labor market limitations	81	100	149	100
None	22	27	60	40
Staff position	19	24	29	20
Experience	26	32	33	22
Small firm	6	7	16	11
Other	8	10	11	7
11. Communication deficiency (yes)	22	27	44	28
12. On-job training (yes)	55	67	99	63
13. Informal assistance	82	100	158	100
Peers	23	28	31	20
Mentors	23	28	32	20
Supervisors	26	32	40	25
Several	—	—	14	9
None	10	12	41	26
14. Rewarding elements of job	82	100	151	100
Confidence in subject	47	57	68	45
Supervisory capability	10	12	12	8
Responsibility, challenge	11	14	28	19
Credibility	6	7	6	4
Personal relationships	1	1	8	5
Other	7	9	29	19

(Table 3–2. continued overleaf)

Table 3-2. continued

Descriptor	Women	% of Women Respondents[a]	Men	% of Men Respondents[a]
15. Disappointing elements of job	84	100	158	100
a. Red tape/bureaucracy	13	16	16	10
b. Excessive travel	2	2	3	2
c. Slow salary increase	–	–	9	6
d. Lack of supervisor competence	2	2	6	4
e. Stress	2	2	–	–
f. Discrimination	5	6	2	1
g. Other/several	50	60	93	59
h. None	10	12	29	18
16. Job satisfaction	82	100	157	100
Very satisfied	37	45	69	44
Above average	6	7	6	4
Average	16	20	27	17
Moderately satisfied	10	12	35	22
Dissatisfied	13	16	20	13
17. Productivity relative to peers	82	100	156	100
Exceptional	17	21	27	17
High	49	60	93	60
Average	16	19	31	20
No peers	–	–	5	3
18. Satisfaction with performance appraisal	82	100	156	100
Very satisfied	30	36	41	26
Satisfied	22	27	60	39
Not satisfied	9	11	20	13
No performance appraisal	21	26	35	22

19. Changes in career path (yes)	27	35	57	58
20. Cope with unanticipated problems (yes)	32	39	51	32
21. Personal change since initial survey	82	100	159	100
Married	10	12	20	13
Separated	—	—	2	1
Divorced	8	10	7	4
Children	5	6	19	12
Health	3	4	5	3
None	44	54	90	57
Other/several	12	15	16	10
22. Integration work/non-work	82	100	158	100
No problem	21	26	81	51
Some problems	60	73	73	46
Many problems	1	1	4	3
23. Impact of job on personal life	82	100	158	100
None	19	23	74	47
Some	46	56	58	37
Significant −	15	18	18	11
Significant +	2	3	8	5
24. Impact of personal life on job	82	100	157	100
None	43	52	110	70
Some	20	24	26	17
Significant −	7	9	7	4
Significant +	12	15	14	9
25. Dual career	79	100	128	100
Positive	12	15	11	9
Some problems	65	82	116	90
No dual career	2	3	1	1

a. Percentages pertain to the number of individuals responding to each question.

after I started the first job. The timetable when I was hired was around 12 to 18 months before a promotion. So I had an early promotion. However, I did not receive a major salary increase with my promotion and geographic shift, because my salary was already out of line with divisional people at the operating facility.

She continues,

I think that job changing is important for people who are on a fast track. If able people don't job hop, they will not move up. In a corporation at the mid-level where most MBAs enter, there is a limit on how fast they will move you because they always try to maintain internal equity. MBAs who are usually above average in ability have to move externally in order to make more money. Companies will have to recognize that more internal movement is desirable. Companies want to recruit high talent people and once they have them in, phase them into the standard corporate population. This is a contradiction in terms.

If people have outstanding performances, you have to treat them specially and they should do this overtly and not camouflage your status, which is what they do. For example, I am excluded from every organization chart because putting me in would disrupt the looks of it. I am in a created job and report up too high. So my status is not overtly defined to anybody. My boss said I was excluded because my reporting relationship was unorthodox and it would not be appropriate to broadcast it. It is important in a corporation to peg everybody.

This Sloan MBA's case may not have been so extreme in the late 1970s when companies attempted to highlight the visibility of women in non-traditional jobs.

Analysis of the entire two-year data set for the years 1977–81 indicates no significant difference in the 52 hours/week worked for women and 51 hours/week for men. For the classes of 1975 and 1976, however, there was a significant difference in the hours per week worked by men and women. Women averaged fifty-four hours per week and males fifty hours per week. The women who entered into non-traditional managerial jobs in the mid-1970s frequently found themselves one of a few such women or the lone woman. Their concern about representing all women managers put them in a double bind. The interviews revealed that some felt that they could not make mistakes. They were fearful of being less than spectacular, and on many tasks they were assigned, there was a tendency to check everything again and again. These women put in long hours convincing themselves that they could do the work.

With the Class of 1977, the male/female hours gap was eliminated. By the end of the 1970s, there were more women working in management. Also, it is likely that the women who selected the Sloan School in the later years were different from their female peers in the classes of 1975 and 1976. The latter Sloans were younger, had less prior work experience, and more closely resembled their male peers in undergraduate education, functional concentration, and their expectations about private sector employment. However, all women, as newcomers in professional management, experienced problems establishing their credibility and perceived more limitations on their mobility within the internal labor market.

Women ranked their lack of specific work experience as the primary constraint on their mobility. Forty percent of the men reported no limitations on their mobility, as compared with 27 percent of the women. Slightly more than a quarter of both men and women reported a communications deficiency. However, men were concerned about their writing skills and women about oral presentations before senior managers who may have been clients. Based on this early finding of communications skills deficiencies, the Sloan School incorporated a series of communications workshops as a part of the core requirement in the Master's Program.

The on-the-job training for two-thirds of the Sloans ranged from two- or three-day orientations to the company culture or one- or two-week specialized courses on a program language, to a twelve- to eighteen-month management trainee program required by some commercial banks. Many were on the fast track or were designated as having high potential, and were placed in shorter programs where they were rotated into several jobs. The adjustments were minimal if Sloans had accepted jobs where they had worked previously. Summer employment between the first and second years of school provided an opportunity for prospective employees to learn the company culture and for employers to assess prospective additions to the work force. Some of the Sloans who went to work in management consulting had worked on a part-time basis with a company during their second year at school.

Surprisingly, a much higher percentage of women than men relied on informal assistance from peers, mentors, and supervisors to perform their jobs. Twenty-six percent of the men and 12 percent of the women indicated that they had no informal assistance. About three-fourths of both men and women rated their productivity as high or exceptional relative to their peers at work, and were over-whelmingly satisfied with their performance appraisal. Almost half of the men and women were very satisfied with their jobs. A higher proportion of women than men noted the confidence they gained by being able to handle the substance in a work setting, which they noted as being the most rewarding element of the job. However, 6 percent of the women who responded to the question on disappoint-ing elements of the job noted sex discrimination. Red tape and bu-reaucracy were the main sources of disappointment for both men and women. Twelve percent of the women and 18 percent of the men reported no disappointing elements of their job.

After this review of the job history of Sloan MBAs two years after graduation, it is not surprising that the difference between the infla-tion-adjusted mean salary of $41,160 for women and $41,550 for men was not significant. Our conclusion was that women after two years earned the same mean salaries as their male peers from Sloan, but also reported greater psychic costs such as more problems in integrating their work and non-work activity; a high negative spill-over of their jobs into their personal lives; and job stress, whereas the men did not. Only 26 percent of the women reported no problems in integrating their work and non-work activities, as compared with 51 percent of the men. Three-fourths of the women reported a spillover of their jobs into their personal lives, usually in a negative fashion, versus 48 percent of the men.

Although the second year questionnaire had not asked about job-related stress, there were many comments on this issue in the open-ended question at the end of the survey. More than half of the second-year responses were made by telephone interviews, which allowed the respondents to discuss at length any issues they consid-ered significant. Dual career marriages also were not included on the two-year survey, but were identified by both women and men as creating additional tensions. As young professionals working a sixty-to eighty-hour week, they did not have the time to devote to new and demanding personal relationships. Some men initially saw such relationships as threatening and opted for working spouses who were "dual-wage earners." Some of their concerns are discussed in Chap-ter 5. The five-year questionnaire—which was designed and tested even as two-year responses were being received—included questions on job-related stress and dual career marriages. Thus, the Sloan MBAs, after two years of "reality shock," had learned a lot about themselves, and had made the transition from full-time graduate student to significant contributors to their organizations. They had more than textbook knowledge of effective decisionmaking in a number of organizations. And, even as soon as two years out of school, women were paying a higher price for an equivalent level of success.

STATUS OF SLOAN MBAs AFTER FIVE YEARS

Eighty-five variables from the five-year follow-up surveys were coded, and revealed that both women and men reported high levels of career and personal success and above average job satisfaction at this stage of their professional development. (See the table in Appendix A; this table is central to the discussion in Chapters 3 through 5 and is presented in a separate appendix.) At five years more than half of the Sloan MBAs had reached middle management, and one-fifth were senior managers. More than three-fourths reported that they were at an organization level commensurate with their training and work experience, and that their job title and compensation were appropriate for someone with their responsibilities.

Respondents were asked how success was measured in their organization and more than 80 percent said that they had been successful with respect to these measures. A slightly lower percentage indicated success with respect to their own measures or goals. Specificity was the rule, especially for males. One male in investment banking stated that when he graduated from Sloan School he expected to earn $200,000 compensation per year by his thirtieth birthday: "I am now 29 years old and I have already reached this objective."

The principal finding of the research is that there were no significant differences between the fifth year compensation of men and women MBAs working full time. Ninety percent of the women worked full time in year five, as did all of the men. Compensation (salary plus bonuses or incentive payment) is widely accepted as the best measure of upward mobility and external career success. Both the scholarly and popular literature note that although female and male MBAs may start their careers at approximately the same salary, as did the Sloan MBAs, the income gap widens over time.[4] The analysis of variance of the fifth year compensation of $49,580 for women and $52,100 for men whows no significant statistical difference, and is thus contrary to the conventional wisdom on this issue. Chapter 5 is devoted to compensation of MBAs and comparisons of Sloan MBAs with graduates of other leading schools of management.

Nevertheless, there are some anomalies in the compensation data. A smaller percent of women (13 percent versus 24 percent) received bonuses; the average amount for a woman was $6,509 as compared with $17,294 for a man. A good part of this differential can be attributed to the key variable, industry of employment. Although approximately the same proportion of men and women worked in the financial services industry (including investment and commercial banking) and the management consulting industries, men were more heavily represented in manufacturing and high technology. Women were more heavily represented in other services such as health services, educational services, and membership organizations. Between the second and the fifth years, this shift away from manufacturing for women placed them in workplaces where bonuses might not have been included in the usual reward structure.

Even where women were equally represented in those industries in which incentive pay is given—management consulting and high technology—their job titles at year five were different from those of males. There were fewer female vice presidents, senior vice presidents, and directors, levels that usually must be attained before a person becomes eligible for a bonus. Between year two and year five over 40 percent of the men had received two or more promotions as compared with 31 percent of the women. Over half of the promotions were made in the manufacturing and high technology industries where males were the predominant workers. (See Table 3–3.)

Men achieved the bonus threshold in two other ways. At least a half dozen males worked in family-owned businesses where they expected to replace their fathers as the chief executive officer. These men started as vice presidents or were quickly promoted into senior management. Also, more males than females worked in overseas assignments where cost-of-living differentials and other financial packages supplemented base salaries. However, the weight of the incentive pay was not sufficient to offset the comparability of base salary for males and females performing similar managerial tasks. Only about 24 percent of the men and 13 percent of the women received bonuses.

The five-year survey might be classified into five major categories: structure of employment, work performance, career success, work

Table 3-3. One or More Promotions for Sloan MBAs by Industry.

Industry	Between Initial and Second Year			Between Second and Fifth Year		
	Total	Women	Men	Total	Women	Men
Manufacturing	46	16	30	38	13	25
High Technology	17	8	9	31	10	21
FIRE	8	3	5	10	1	9
Management Consulting	26	11	15	23	7	16
Public Sector	8	4	4	4	2	2
Other Services	7	4	3	13	7	6
Investment Banking	3	2	1	3	1	2
Commercial Banking	15	5	10	11	4	7
Military	—	—	—	2	—	2
Total	130	53	77	135	45	90

relationships, and personal life. Detailed statistics are in Appendix A. Several of the important mobility indicators will be discussed here. Structure of employment defines the internal labor market and includes industry, job titles, job descriptions, level in the organization, job classification, change of functions, and change of employers since the second year survey. Respondents provided detailed answers on job descriptions and the parameters of middle management for their companies. On the former, they submitted job specifications from personnel files and on the latter, tables of organizations, in which they noted their locations in the company hierarchy and the number of levels and grades that separated them from the chief executive officer. We shall examine two subgroups of employment structure which are developed more extensively in the section on mobility indicators. Industry of employment is reviewed in a separate chapter. Change of functions and change of employers underlie the dynamics of upward mobility.

Change of Functions

Although almost half of both men and women had changed their functions between years two and five, their status differed as a result of these changes. Function changes for men were usually accompanied by promotions and upgraded responsibilities. They shifted out of finance and into strategic planning or marketing. Reasons given for the changes were "needed to gain broader experience; interesting opportunity; more money; wanted line responsibility." Women mainly changed job functions to accommodate changes in their personal lives. After returning from maternity leave, some requested assignments where the schedules were lighter or travel required less frequently. A few changed to less demanding routines after serious illnesses. When women relocated geographically, to be with their spouses, they frequently changed functions on their new jobs. However, more men than women changed functions at high salaries as they left management consulting, and more men than women changed functions as they became entrepreneurs. At the end of five years many Sloan MBAs were based in marketing, migrating there mainly from finance.

Change of Employers

Respondents to the five-year survey were asked if they had changed employers within the past three years, and the name of their former employer, dates of change, and reasons for these changes. These changes were external to the firm, representing both intra- and inter-industry shifts. Reversing their action of the first two years, women now changed employers more than men. Only 42 percent of the men changed employers compared with 56 percent of the women. Why did women move more frequently than men during the latter part of the five-year period? Some moves might be attributed to the women's dual career status. Ninety percent of the married women reported a dual career relationship—they were frequently trailing spouses in the geographic relocation of the household. Their spouses tended to be further along in their careers and were the more significant earners.

Women who changed industries between years two and five received a significantly lower salary increase than did men. We speculate that women have changed jobs even at lower salary levels for reasons related to the work environment. At least 70 percent of the women reported that they had to modify their personal behavior, goals, and ideas to "fit" in their organizations. Among the explanations listed by women for modifying behavior were: "changed hairstyle and dress; toned-down behavior; tempered my aggression; as the only woman and only MBA must tone down in order to fit; must conform to conservative group norms; low-key style; tone down myself in order to deal with peers; need to be more competitive in order to survive; had to become more political and less outspoken; more reserved and less risk taking; must turn the other cheek." What was unusual was that a number of the women responded by stating that they had to "tone down," and not a single male used this term. What may have occurred as these young women moved into non-traditional jobs in management was a denial of their femininity. They gave up color in their clothes, flair in their style, and tried not to draw attention to the fact that they were young, articulate, and talented. They became "grey ladies."

The women may have pursued this path because relatively more women than men had job credibility problems. Sixty-four percent of the men reported no job credibility problems, while only 43 percent of the women said they had no problems gaining or maintaining credibility in the performance of their jobs. Women reported reasons for credibility problems such as: "being female and working in a predominately male environment; a young woman in a job ordinarily done by a male; had to deal with the young, inexperienced female syndrome; lacked executive experience; female and young; I look younger than most at my level."

When men discussed some modifications of their behavior they noted such things as slowing down their pace; learning to be more patient; curbing their entrepreneurial spirit; and learning to delegate more responsibility. Men modified their behavior also because they thought they were being perceived as elitist, arrogant, or intolerant, or because they needed more time to move up a steep learning curve or to overcome the perception of being a "technical jock."

Career Success

Assessing career success involves examining opportunities for upward mobility through progression paths, number of promotions, performance appraisals, and job satisfaction. The analysis of variance indicates six areas where the differences between men and women were significant and where women MBAs have experienced difficulties.

Maintaining job credibility and behavior modification have been discussed above. Progression paths, sex of the supervisor, mentors, and changed aspirations were the remaining four variables. Mentoring is discussed in Chapter 5, where it is examined as one of the determinants of fifth year MBA compensation.

The fifth year questionnaire asked Sloan graduates to define the usual progression path for those in their position in their company; to specify the time frame for this progression; and to indicate whether they were on track in accordance with this time frame. Sixty-one percent of the men compared to 54 percent of the women (a significant difference) reported that they were on track in accordance with the internal labor market requirements of their companies. Did women MBAs underestimate their career development? The following diagram outlines the career success responses and reasons for lagging behind a perceived time frame.

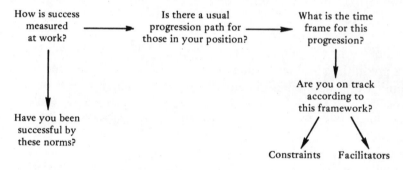

Where Sloan MBAs lagged behind a perceived time frame, they reported constraints on their progress, and nearly two-fifths noted some personal shortcoming was involved. Women responded that "being a woman or being female were 'real' barriers to further progress." Their personal lives also interfered with career development. One Sloan woman responded, "I find that my professional progress seems less important than my eight month old son's development, at least for the time being." Personal constraints identified by men were health, unwillingness to relocate, personal motivation, and desire to start their own companies.

Sloan MBAs were severely critical when they faulted the rules of the internal labor market. One male who had accepted an initial job in the information system department of an investment bank was permitted to transfer to the investment banking side of the organization as an associate, after one year on the job. He was later informed that his year in the staff job would not be counted toward the four-year period an associate was expected to serve before being promoted to vice president. By the time of his fifth year survey he had achieved a high salary, received a large bonus and an outstanding performance appraisal, but had one more year of apprenticeship before being promoted. He was told that an argument for early promotion (that is short of four years in this current position) could not be made, that this was a decision dictated by number of years and to make an exception would be very difficult.

Promotions

Ninety percent of the women, as compared with 80 percent of the men, reported receiving at least one promotion between years two and five. It might appear that women were outpacing men in promotions during the last part of the five-year period. However, another way to examine the promotions is to note that of the 135 promotions reported between years two and five, women (who make up about one-third of the sample) received one-third of the promotions and men, two-thirds. The promotions were primarily in manufacturing, high technology, and management consulting; see Table 3-3. Since 20 percent of the men and only 10 percent of the women did not receive a promotion, it is likely that one of the other upward mobility indicators camouflaged the number of real promotions— for example, the shift out of the corporate structure into entrepreneurship. One male Sloan MBA, after a short tenure in a real estate subsidiary of an investment banking firm, served as president of an aging warehousing and distribution facility. By the time of his fifth year follow-up survey, he had become co-owner of a $400 million office complex and was later profiled in *Business Week.*

The other variables that were significantly different between male and female Sloan MBAs were changed aspirations and mentors. Approximately three-fifths of the women had changed their career aspirations, while slightly less than half of the men had done so. Whereas an overwhelming percentage of the males had defined their aspirations more precisely, women were almost evenly split between lowering and increasing their aspirations. Some women were pleasantly surprised as their careers evolved, and they became more knowl-

edgeable about the opportunities. Others tried to find balance between their personal and professional lives and lowered their aspirations. Lowered expectations might account for the fact that 90 percent of the women as compared with 70 percent of the men were
satisfied with their performance appraisals.

Activities in the personal lives of the women frequently interfered
with their jobs. Slightly more married males and more male Sloan
MBAs with children reported in the survey. The men with children
mostly relied on spouses at home for child care arrangements; women
with children relied on various combinations of sitters, day care, and
schools. Working mothers spent 3 hours per week during the work
week with their children, and the males spent 2.3 hours. Although
males in dual career relationships reported that most of their spouses
had not progressed as far in their careers, women who reported were
married to successful spouses who had progressed as far if not further than their wives. Even in these successful dual careers more
women felt that their careers were constrained by the professional
activities of their spouses. Dual career relations are discussed more
fully in Chapter 5.

Five years into their postgraduate careers, the Sloan MBAs remained achievement-oriented, highly motivated, and their own
harshest critics. Throughout the ten-year data collection phase, they
asked for status reports on the preliminary findings for their class.
Although they were successful in their respective organizations, they
wanted to measure their success against their Sloan School classmates. About two-thirds of both men and women reported above
average to excellent job satisfaction.

There were no significant differences in fifth year compensation
between men and women Sloan MBAs, but the comparable economic
achievement was attained at greater psychic costs for women. A
larger proportion of women than men reported some problems with
job credibility, as noted previously in this chapter. At the time of the
five-year survey, both men and women indicated that four-fifths of
their co-workers were male while 84 percent of the supervisors of the
women were male as compared with 96 percent of the supervisors of
males. More women were supervising other women, especially in the
other service industries such as health and education. Nevertheless,
the managerial workplaces of the 1980s still were dominated by
males.

Perhaps the best measures of differences in psychic costs for men and women are revealed in the hours of work per week and in job-related stress. In the early years of the research there was a significant difference between men and women in hours of work after two years. Sloan women MBAs from the first three classes (1975 through 1977) apparently had a more difficult time adjusting to their nontraditional jobs. In the interviews, they discussed the problems of representing a gender group, rather than the problems of being accepted as individual performers. Several were told by their supervisors that other women MBAs had failed and thus the probability of their survival was low. In such a work environment, women may have devoted considerably more time to performing tasks for which they were well equipped. There was the fear that if they performed poorly, all women MBAs would be judged negatively.

Our interim report (July 1979) on the two-year survey for the Classes of 1975 and 1976 indicates that 74 percent of the women, compared with 59 percent of the men, worked more than fifty hours per week. A later report covering the Classes of 1975–77 showed 54.2 hours/week for women and 50.5 hours/week for men, a significant difference. Women in subsequent classes were better able to deal with being singled out for special scrutiny in the workplace. Other women had proceeded them, hence they were not the token pioneers. Supervisors were beginning to be less openly antagonistic or less skeptical about the performance of women. Women in the Classes of 1978 and 1979 averaged the same number of work hours per week as their male peers. Having mastered a normal hours/week schedule at year two contributed to the adjustment of these women during the next three years. By year five, full-time workers among women and men averaged a fifty-two hours/week schedule.

Job-related stress was not explicitly included on the two-year survey, but Tilney's review of the same data in a master's thesis at Sloan showed detailed comments and discussion of poor physical health conditions.[5] These two-year responses were coded and scaled (1 to 5) (see Table 3–4) and at the same time a series of questions were pre-tested for inclusion in the five-year survey. At year five, Sloan women MBAs appear to pay a higher price to obtain a comparable salary level because they are under a significantly higher level of stress than the men. More detailed comments on stress are included in Chapter 5.

Table 3-4. Stress Levels for Male and Female MBAs.

Variable	Problems Related to Stress (1 = little, 5 = lots)		Stress Affecting Personal Life (1 = little, 5 = lots)	
	Male	Female	Male	Female
Mean	2.31	2.95	1.66	2.14
t value (pool variance estimate)	3.58		2.73	

SPECIAL SUBGROUPS

Throughout this chapter, the major comparisons of Sloan MBAs have been between men and women graduates. The professional progress of three other subgroups requires some attention. Chapter 6 will provide a detailed analysis of the progress of one subgroup, minority Sloans, during the five-year period. The fifty-two white males from the Classes of 1975 and 1976 (the Short Fives) have not been included in the preceding statistical review. But the few postdoctoral MBAs are included in the aggregate data since they, like other students in the two-year program, received the SM degree, and except for being slightly older, they did not differ from other Sloan MBAs.

Eight individuals—one of the subgroups—in the Sloan School sample were graduated from the Master's Program in Management after having received a doctorate in another discipline. These individuals were mainly assistant professors who changed careers because of low probabilities of tenure, disenchantment with the academic lifestyle, or some personal crisis, such as a divorce. Physical science, engineering, law, and the humanities were their fields of previous employment. Several of the more technically trained said that they were channeled into narrow job slots where they would be less likely to move into general management. The lawyers used their dual credentials in specialties such as international management and finance. The liberal arts doctorates accepted jobs in which they utilized skills acquired in their management school concentrations. As Tenenbaum found in her study of postdoctorate MBAs, these individuals were less attractive to most potential employers than their less highly credentialed classmates.[6] Nevertheless, at the end of five years, these postdoctorate Sloan MBAs were generally as successful as their Sloan School peers.

The initial profile of the Short Fives matched that of other male Sloan graduates in 1975 and 1976 except that a slightly higher percentage had undergraduate majors in engineering and more concentrated in management information systems (MIS) operations research. This is not surprising given that the objective of the match between men and women was on the basis of comparable background. Women graduates from the first two classes differed in academic background from their male peers. Like all male Sloan MBAs, these men, five years later, were married, had children, worked mostly in manufacturing and high technology at upper middle management, and were very satisfied with their jobs. After five years, their salaries were only slightly (and not significantly) higher than for all male Sloan MBAs ($51,216 versus $50,300, not adjusted for inflation).

CONCLUSION

After five years of postgraduate work experiences, a different type of manager emerged from the Sloan School MBAs. Although they had been promoted into upper middle management, some into senior management, and had received significant gains in compensation, they were primarily contributors. Even with nearly half changing their functions between the second and fifth years, they worked at senior levels as directors of long range planning or strategic planning, senior vice presidents of finance and planning, marketing managers, partners or principals in management consulting, vice presidents in acquisitions and mergers in investment banking, and managers of information system planning. The division into staff and line functions does not seem to be appropriate for this group—they were senior specialists and professionals who supervised about three persons. A decade ago Peter Keen noted that "the role of specialist in business has grown immensely and while it may still be true that senior executives remain generalists in their orientation, they increasingly draw on a range of professional, technical, and staff personnel who have substantial impact on the organization's decision making and who are also now reaching senior positions within the management hierarchy."[7] The Sloan MBAs from the classes of 1975-79 seem to be on this career path. To some extent, they are the forerunners of the management types of the 1990s, individuals who work easily with new technology and the increasing complexities of their organizations.

Another outcome that was not unexpected was the shift away from large corporate bureaucracies to smaller enterprises and into more entrepreneurial activities. Sloans were individuals who opted to attend a small management school (graduating classes of under 150 persons during their tenure) and may have preferred smaller scale workplaces because they felt more comfortable there. Many stated that small organizations appealed to them because they were less impersonal, more flexible, and provided better opportunities for career development.

Yet, a divergence had emerged between the achievements of men and women during the latter part of the five-year period. Men had migrated into manufacturing and high technology industries, and women moved into other service industries. Relatively fewer women believed that they were on track in accordance with the progression paths for their jobs in their companies. More women than men had job credibility problems after five years, and significantly more women had to modify their behavior in order to fit into their organizations. Thus, significantly more women experienced job-related stress. Based on these differences, after five years of work, we anticipate that female MBAs will have to cope with even more problems in the future.

NOTES

1. The "tournament model of career systems describes a career selection system as a series of implicit competitions which progressively differentiate a cohort of employers, throughout their careers, each time further defining their opportunities for future attainments," James E. Rosenbaum, *Career Mobility in a Corporate Hierarchy* (Orlando, Fla.: Academic Press, 1984), p. 27.

2. John Veiga, "Mobility Influences During Managerial Career Stages," *Academy of Managemant Journal* 26 (1983): 74-85.

3. John P. Kotter, *Power and Influence* (New York: The Free Press, 1985), p. 45.

4. Mary Anne Devanna, *Male/Female Careers: The First Decade* (New York: Columbia University, Graduate School of Business, 1984); Myra Strober, "The MBA: Same Passport to Success for Women and Men?" in P.A. Wallace, ed., *Women in the Workplace* (Boston : Auburn House Publishing Co., 1982), pp. 25–44. Josephine E. Olson, Irene H. Frieze, and Deborah C. Good, "The Effects of Job Type and Industry On the Income of Male and Female MBAs," *Journal of Human Resources* 22 (Fall 1987): 532–41.

5. Cathleen Tilney, "Stress and MBA's," Master's thesis, Sloan School at MIT, June 1982.

6. Elizabeth Brody Tenenbaum, "The Post-Doctoral MBA: A Study in Career Change," Master's thesis, Sloan School of Management at MIT, June 1982.

7. Peter Keen, "Cognitive Style and Career Specialization," in J. Van Maanen, ed., *Organizational Careers: Some New Perspectives* (New York: John Wiley and Sons, 1977), p. 89.

4 INDUSTRY OF EMPLOYMENT OF SLOAN SCHOOL GRADUATES

Industry of employment is one of the significant determinants of upward mobility of the young managers who graduated from the Sloan School. The statistical analysis of fifth year compensation discussed in the next chapter also emphasizes the importance of industry of employment. Our study analyzed industry-specific employment patterns of Sloan MBAs by converting the more than 700 employers reported by survey respondents into Standard Industrial Classification (SIC) codes, based on the primary activities of the companies as documented in a number of sources such as Standard and Poor's, and Dun and Bradstreet.[1] These SIC codes were then classified into nine industry groups: manufacturing; high technology; finance, insurance, and real estate (the acronym FIRE is used); management consulting; public/non-profit sector; other services; investment banking; commercial banking; and the military. Table 4-1 shows the number of full-time employed persons by each industry.

INDUSTRY STRUCTURE

Some of the mobility changes of the Sloans would have been obscured if the standard manufacturing and non-manufacturing definitions had been used. The methodology for classification of industry groups was not established at the beginning of the research, but

Table 4-1. Full-Time Employed Sloan MBAs by Industry (*percent of total*).

Industry n =	Initial Survey			Two-Year Survey			Five-Year Survey[a]		
	Total (306)	Men (197)	Women (109)	Total (244)	Men (159)	Women (85)	Total (195)	Men (128)	Women (67)
Manufacturing, Mining and Construction	28.1	26.9	30.3	32.0	35.2	25.9	23.5	26.6	17.9
High Technology	14.0	15.7	11.0	15.6	17.0	12.9	22.0	23.4	19.4
Finance, Insurance, Real Estate	8.2	9.6	5.5	6.1	6.3	5.9	7.7	9.3	4.5
Management Consulting	23.5	23.3	23.8	22.9	20.7	27.1	18.5	17.2	20.9
Government/Non-Profit	2.0	1.0	3.7	6.1	6.3	5.9	4.1	3.9	4.5
Other Services	11.4	12.2	10.1	8.6	6.9	11.8	13.3	9.4	20.9
Investment Banking	1.3	1.0	1.8	1.6	1.3	2.3	2.6	3.1	1.5
Commercial Banking	10.8	9.1	13.8	7.0	6.3	8.2	7.2	5.5	10.4
Military	0.6	1.0	—	—	—	—	1.0	1.6	—

a. Adjustments were not made for non-respondents where industry of employment is known.

rather evolved over time as we received detailed information on job titles, job descriptions, progression paths, and other internal labor market characteristics. Appendix C provides the names of selected private sector employers of Sloan School graduates. Because of the considerable number of mergers and acquisitions during the latter part of the data collection period, no attempt was made to re-classify employers. For example, an individual employed by Electronic Data Services (EDS) in year two would be included in the high technology sector and would remain in high technology at year five, even though EDS had been acquired by General Motors, a manufacturing concern. Also, an employee of Dean Witter Reynolds would remain in the financial services industry, even after this firm's acquisition by Sears, a retailer.

Since almost half of the Sloan students had majored in engineering, natural sciences, and mathematics in their undergraduate curricula, jobs in high technology industries had special appeal, attracting 14 percent of the initial survey respondents and 22 percent after five years. Usually high technology is embedded in the manufacturing sector, but selected manufacturing and service groups were combined into a more precise category to track the progress of the Sloan MBAs.[2] The percentage of MBAs who were employed in financial services, encompassing finance, insurance, and real estate ranged from 6–8 percent throughout the five-year period. But we have shown commercial and investment banking as separate industrial groups. These two groups, plus FIRE, accounted for 20 percent of the initial employment, 15 percent after two years, and 17 percent by the fifth year.

For Sloan graduates, compensation in investment banking was more than double what was received in commercial banking by year five. Progression paths were quite different in the two industries. One employee of a major investment bank reported that the typical individual was hired as an associate and expected to remain in that job category, with merit salary increases and bonuses, for a four-year period, before being eligible to be a vice president. Then within a ten-year period, one could be promoted to partner. In this relatively flat hierarchy, unusual individuals or fast trackers could beat this timetable. Commercial banking, on the other hand, had layers of senior management and a wider range for middle management levels. Thus, we have separated the financial sector into three groups: commercial banking, investment banking, and other finance, insurance, and real

Table 4-2. Five Years Later–Sloan School Graduates of the Same Class in Commercial Banking.

Descriptors	Female	Male
Full-time work prior to Sloan School	2 years, 7 months	0
Sloan School concentration	Planning and control	Finance
Age at Graduation	25 years	23 years
Initial employer	Same large commercial bank	Same large commercial bank
Initial job title	Assistant to SVP operations	Management trainee (commercial lending)
Initial salary	$21,000–23,500 →	$19,000–22,000 →
Two-year job title	Assistant Treasurer commercial accounts operations	Assistant Treasurer lease financing
Two-year salary	$25,000 + bonus	$26,500 + bonus
Promotions	1) Initial job + 12 months 2) Initial job + 24 months 3) Initial job + 30 months	1) Initial job + 13 months 2) Initial job + 24 months 3) Initial job + 36 months 4) Initial job + 48 months
Five-year job title	Assistant VP (commercial paper operations)	Vice President of leasing/financing
Five-year base salary	$52,000 + bonus	$70,000 + bonus of 50–100% base salary

estate (FIRE). Few Sloan graduates worked in insurance and real estate, but they were represented in the burgeoning financial services industry.

With so many structural shifts in the financial services industry, it was possible for two Sloan graduates in the same class to begin their employment in commercial banking, and five years later to work for the same employer in different areas at significantly different salaries. One Sloan graduate worked on the retail side of the organization in commercial banking, and one was on the institutional or asset management side of the organization. Table 4-2 delineates the different experiences of these two graduates. The $18,000 differential in their fifth year base salaries reflected that they were operating in different segments of the financial services industry. The woman was employed in more traditional commercial banking activities and as an assistant vice president on the retail side, earned $52,000 plus a bonus. The man was employed as vice president of leasing finance and received a salary of $70,000 plus a bonus of from 50–100 percent of base salary. His responsibilities were comparable to the types of activities in investment banking, so the employer had to meet labor market prices of investment, not commercial banking.

Management consulting was one of the most important industries for both the entry of new graduates and their exodus from it over a five-year period. The official definition (SIC 7392) of this industry was expanded to include those individuals who performed consulting activities in other industrial settings. Several of the large accounting firms hired Sloan graduates to work in their management consulting divisions, rather than in accounting and auditing services (SIC 893). Job descriptions, job titles, and other criteria indicated that these individuals were performing tasks identical to their counterparts in management consulting firms. An article in December 4, 1984 edition of *The Wall Street Journal* noted that Touche Ross and Co., a "Big Eight" accounting firm, had acquired Braxton, Inc., one of the ten largest independent management consulting firms in the United States. The article read, in part: "While the eight largest accounting firms have in-house consulting practices, this is the first time that a major U.S. CPA firm has acquired an outside major consulting practice. . . . About 15 percent of Touche Ross's current revenue is derived from its internal management consulting practice. Arthur Andersen and Co., the biggest U.S. CPA firm, gets 28 percent of its revenue from management consulting."[3] In 1987, another article in *The New York Times* noted that the fastest growing part of many accounting firms was management consulting; in that article a "Big Eight" partner indicated that 21 percent of the professionals at his firm worked at consulting compared with 12 percent five years ago.[4]

Almost one-fourth of the Sloan graduates from the classes of 1975–79 accepted positions in the management consulting industry. Nearly 60 percent of this initial group later left this industry; however, they were replaced by others who entered consulting after starting in other industries. At year five, even with an excess of exits over entries, management consulting still accounted for 19 percent of the full-time employment of Sloan MBAs. With an average starting salary of $36,000 (adjusted for inflation), management consulting offered the second highest beginning salary of any industrial group. Even in year five, when the salary of $55,000 ranked third behind investment banking and financial services, it was above the fifth year average salary of $51,000 for all Sloan full-time employees.

Two industrial groups deserve additional comment here. The category "other services" is a collection of miscellaneous services such as legal, educational, health, and labor unions. Over the five-year period this category accounted for 9 to 13 percent of Sloan graduates' employment. The military, though it accounts for few Sloan graduates, in absolute numbers, has been specified as an industry group as distinct from public service (this, because throughout the time the surveys were conducted, a few military personnel attended Sloan School on a full-time basis, received the master's degree, and resumed their military careers). In the statistical analysis of fifth year compensation of males and females, the prior work experience variable was significant for males, but not for females. More than 10 percent of the males had been military officers and sought the management degree to smooth their transition into the civilian sector.

Twenty-eight percent of the Sloan MBAs accepted jobs in manufacturing industries. The retention rate for this industry was 64 percent in year two, but declined to 49 percent between the second and the fifth years. Only 38 percent of those who started out in this industry remained by the fifth year. The retention rate is the percentage of individuals employed in an industry, in some base period, who had remained in that industry. It is likely that the true manufacturing retention rate was higher, since high technology and manufacturing industries were treated as a separate industrial category. The migration of persons between the high technology and manufacturing sectors was significant. Combining the two industry groups shows that the more inclusive manufacturing industry accounts for slightly more than two-fifths of employment throughout the five-year period. Because Sloan students who concentrated in finance, planning and control, and management information systems accounted for four-fifths of the Sloan graduates, their manufacturing jobs upon graduation tended to be staff jobs in corporate offices rather than on the plant floor. The job titles that predominated in the initial year for those in manufacturing were financial analyst, business analyst, staff assistant, product manager, materials manager, manufacturing cost analyst, and product planning analyst.

The industrial classifications exclude the nine part-time workers who were present only in the fifth year, they were mainly women with small children. The part-time workers, full-time students, and unemployed individuals accounted for a small percent of the respondents, and have been excluded from detailed analysis.

In Chapter 3, 321 respondents were reported in the initial year, of which 306 were full-time employees. Fifteen persons were either students, unemployed, or not in the labor force. In the second year there were 244 full-time employees out of 251 respondents, and year five had 195 full-time employees out of 219 respondents. Two individuals who worked on a full-time basis in occupations not generally associated with business have also been excluded. One individual was a general reporter on a small newspaper, and another has become a prolific author of paperback novels. Other individuals who worked as managers in private nonprofit agencies were included in the industrial category, public, and nonprofit industries.

The pattern of industrial employment in the initial year partly reflects the role of the Sloan School placement office. Nearly all of the Sloan graduates accepted job offers from companies who re-recruited on campus. The fact that nearly two-thirds of the students had concentrated in finance, and planning and control, attracted employers seeking individuals with these skills. The relative importance in employment of each industrial group over the five-year period may be associated more with opportunities for advancement within different organizations. Table 4-1 revealed that initially, male and female graduates were distributed in about the same proportion in the nine industry groups. This distributional pattern provided the underpinning for the inter-industry shifts over the next five years. With relatively high retention rates from one-third to one-half by year five, it is apparent that the primary finding—full-time women employees had performed as well as their male peers—is associated with similar patterns of employment by industry.

Women students who received the master's degree in management during the period 1975–79 accepted jobs mainly in management consulting, manufacturing, high technology, commercial banking, and other services, as did their male Sloan School peers. Five years later the distribution by industry was not altered significantly, except that men had reduced their presence in commercial banking and other services, two of the lowest paying private sector industries. Both men and women were well represented in manufacturing, management consulting, and high technology. Other studies of MBA salaries have shown significant differences in the salaries of men and women, because they work in different industries.[5] More women are usually employed in public sector jobs or, if in comparable private sector industries, in staff jobs. Neither is true for Sloan women graduates.

Management consulting and the role of women in this industry, some special difficulties that women have experienced in manufacturing industries, and an analysis of mobility across industries and job changes within industries are the topics of the remainder of this chapter. The case studies in management consulting and manufacturing, two industries which accounted for approximately two-thirds of employment for the Sloan graduates, describe the unique work experience of women and how they were treated differently in these labor markets.

MANAGEMENT CONSULTING

Management consulting, a relatively new industry, attracted MBAs in the late 1970s and early 1980s. According to the Bureau of Labor Statistics, employment in this industry increased 72 percent between 1975 and 1980. One consulting firm, which employed 10 percent of the Sloan graduates in management consulting, grew from a base of 5 persons in 1978 to 175 by 1981. MBAs were hired as junior consultants or associates and unlike other entry level jobs, as much emphasis was placed on team work as on individual effort. Yet these positions required more entrepreneurial finesse than comparable corporate jobs. Much of the work is project oriented, with individual employee evaluations made after the conclusion of each project. Typical responsibilities at this level include data collection ("numbers crunching"), report writing, and limited interaction with clients.

Skills from functional areas—marketing, finance, strategic planning, and organizational development—are combined. One of the Sloan respondents noted that in addition to the technical skills needed for the job, the common denominator was "basic smarts" and the ability to organize, quickly grasp the situation, and analyze it. Both written and oral communication skills are essential. Because of the project-to-project nature of the assignments, there is a limited amount of developmental opportunity. Another Sloan respondent wrote, "Everything seems to be happenstance. There is a lack of control over the type of job that you are on as well as exposure to a given officer of the organization. If you are fortunate, you find one officer who is a focal point and hope to work with him most of the time. Praise is not strongly forthcoming. It took me almost a year to deal with that mode of operation."

Project director, or case leader is the next level of responsibility. These individuals have the responsibility for the day-to-day direction of projects. They manage professionals, interview senior managers within client organizations, plan and budget, and make oral and written presentations for the client's senior management. This rank was usually reached by Sloan MBAs within two years of their initial employment.

Such levels of responsibility entailed considerable travel, since management consulting firms may be highly specialized (the so-called boutique firms), and service clients nationally and sometimes on a worldwide basis. Both men and women complained about the exhausting and excessive travel. The necessity to travel so frequently and to operate on a minimum seventy-hour work week did not encourage long-term employment in the industry.

The probability of becoming a principal, or partner, the top professional level usually reached after five or six years, is low in management consulting because of the flat management structure. The typical management consulting firms had 200 or fewer employees, and the age of the founding partners may have been about forty years. The turnover after two years was considerable. However, the respondents, although exceptionally well compensated with salary and bonuses, noted that not just the lack of opportunity for upward mobility was responsible for the turnover. Some left the industry because they needed something more tangible—that after a while, the interaction with clients was no longer challenging. Others said that they were frustrated because there were few opportunities to implement the recommendations they made to clients. One individual termed himself a "corporate voyeur." The major reason given by both men and women for leaving the industry was that there was little technical and intellectual requirements of much of the work.

Given the relatively high retention rate of about 40 percent over a five-year period in this industry, what were the motivators for those who continued to work as consultants? Respondents noted that salary advances occurred at high, regular rates, as long as the consultant billed a certain number of hours to clients. Thus, salary improvement might be decoupled from professional advancement in title and responsibility. Some individuals served as project directors for years. Several of the larger, more established management consulting firms, however, followed a strict "up or out" practice as they replaced junior consultants with the eager graduates from the business schools.

The profiles of the six women Sloan graduates who were employed in management consulting highlights the problems of upward mobility in an industry with two to four year apprentice period. Two of the women reached the project director level and left for jobs in manufacturing and other services, respectively. Three remained in the industry and eventually reached the senior position of principal and/or partner. One minority woman started in the industry and after a number of difficulties left to work for a small minority firm. Three of the women had majored in mathematics in undergraduate school; of the remaining three, one each majored in engineering, the social sciences, and natural science. With one exception, they had concentrated in finance and/or planning and control while at the Sloan School. Not a single minority male was employed in the management consulting industry. The statements in the following case studies are direct quotes from the several surveys completed by Sloan MBAs.

We followed the development of each woman at discrete points over the five-year period and could assess her performance against the expected progression path for management consulting—junior consultant, project director, and principal.

Case A: Reached Senior Consultant Level and Left the Industry (Exit)

Two-Year Survey. I am still an associate consultant. My bonuses have been in the top end of the scale, higher than average, but I have not been promoted. Although my primary manager spent a lot of time telling me what the environment was and how to work within it, he did not support my promotion. I have heard from several sources, both people who were and were not involved in the decision that the reason for not being promoted was because I was a female. There are about 160 professionals in this office and only three women.

Officially, I was told that I was lacking in certain experiences, particularly project management, client management, and interfacing. Another reason, I believe, is that the company is trying to lengthen the time frame for making partner. Historically, they have had an average new partner age of thirty-three, and they want to raise that to thirty-six. I am too young, as yet, but I feel that I am ready. The male/female relationship has been the most difficult, particularly with people who have not dealt at all with professional women. Professionally, I did not expect sexism to hold me back when the chips were down. I had a problem with one of my managers who did not know how to deal with women, especially since this job requires frequent travel with male colleagues. Fifty percent of my time has been spent on the road. With a third person, we discussed where you draw the line between a social and a business relationship.

Five-Year Survey. Shortly after I was promoted from associate consultant to senior consultant (two years ago) at my previous employer, I left for a job in the corporate sector as manager of operations analysis, a middle management job in my firm. I am eligible for bonuses and have gotten the salary increases that I wanted to get. I have successfully completed the major projects assigned to me and received positive feedback. At my level, there is only one other woman who was recently promoted. I expect a promotion within the next six months.

When the promotion was made, it was a significant one to director, which tracks into senior management.

Case B: Reached Project Director and Left the Industry (Exit)

First Year Survey. I was one of five professional women in my firm (200 professionals) and felt that I was treated very much like the other new men in the firm. I also found that my young age did not hinder credibility, and my salary was increased 17 percent after ten months. I think that one's level of stamina could be a determining factor for mobility. Ease of movement seems to be a function of intelligence and "politicking."

Two-Year Survey. I have received salary increases in connection with high performance. One salary increase was extremely high in order to realign my salary with other professionals who were older. Although my salary has increased 70 percent over my beginning salary, two years ago, I am only moderately satisfied with my job. There are two problems in consulting: (a) One must start at the beginning with every client in terms of learning about his

business before one can build a conceptual base for looking across businesses;
(b) The traveling involved is exhausting and disruptive to one's life. Intellectually, I knew that there would be problems in being a woman consultant,
but the real difference is in experiencing the problems rather than knowing
about them.

Five-Year Survey.   After two and a half years, I left consulting because of the
travel demands and because I wanted to implement some of the strategies
that I had recommended. I am Director of Corporate Planning, a senior position in my present company, and I am the most senior woman. I am perceived as a competent professional with excellent training in strategic planning. I am also perceived as aggressive, but I have learned to temper my
aggression.

These two women management consultants left the industry after
three years. Each has been exceedingly successful in other industries.
The excessive travel (more than 50 percent of the time) and the standard sixty- to seventy-hour work week eventually took its toll. Both
women entered management consulting in the late 1970s, when
women consultants were hardly visible. Although both received commendations from their clients, indicating that they were regarded as
highly competent, they had some problems with males in their firms.
Each had chosen consulting because she was not certain what she
wanted to do. After a few years, it became evident that each wanted
to work in the corporate structure—perhaps, each gained a perspective in management consulting that enabled her to be quite successful
later. Lateral entry into middle management from consulting may
have placed them at a higher level than they might have reached if
the initial position had been an entry level job with their second
employers.

An 1981 article in *Business Week* stated that substantial numbers
of women discovered consulting was a short-cut to corporate achievement and a way of bypassing lower managerial jobs. Management
consulting had long been a springboard to lofty corporate positions
for men as far back as the 1960s, and a handful of women also used
it to move up in corporations. The article also noted that for women,
as for men, the key advantage is the versatility a management consultant develops in a relatively short time. Moreover, by working at the
strategic level across many industries, consultants become adept
problem solvers and quick studies at many subjects, a process that
teaches them to think as does top management. One of the Sloan

School graduates included in our management consulting sample is profiled in the article.[7]

The next cases follow the activities of three women who remained in the management consulting industry and eventually reached the senior status of principal.

Case C: Remained in Industry and Worked at Several Consulting Firms Before Becoming Principal

First Year Survey. My salary was increased 29 percent, and I expected to be promoted within six months. Nevertheless, I was passed over as a project manager on a major assignment. I was told that the client was uncomfortable with a woman. The most difficult aspect of my job has been achieving some strangely accepted and required balance of so-called femininity and aggressiveness. It is quite clear that the bravado and toughness apparent in many of the young male consultants (and admired by some partners) is considered truly offensive in young women consultants. At the same time, there is the hazard of appearing too "demure," insecure, retiring, etc. It seems to require an almost constant testing out of behaviors.

Two-Year Survey. I was promoted to senior consultant (project director) a year and a half into the job. I have seen incredible growth on my part, in terms of functional skills, confidence levels, industry level. It has been an upward sloping learning curve that has not leveled out for me. The only disappointments are that the amount of travel and the volume of work have gone beyond any expectations that I had when I accepted the job. Clients on the whole have been receptive to me as a woman, and I have built strong, good professional relationships with them. I am in line for a top management position and see that within the next five years. I do not have a commanding physical presence, and I think that has a real bearing on how people react to me, and deal with me. That surprised me.

Five-Year Survey. I was promoted to Associate (one level below principal) after four years. I have just received a 35 percent salary increase, but no promotion. I have decided to leave the firm, since the company has now revised the entire position hierarchy and lengthened the period to be promoted to partnership. When I entered, people were making partner in four to five years. Now, the time frame is ten years. In order to be promoted to principal and into partnership, the decision must be unanimous by partners within a given division. My boss proposed that I be promoted, but two partners cast negative votes.

I have been successful, gained credibility with my clients, built a lot of technical skills and have a strong reputation in the field, external to my company. Nevertheless, I have been negatively rated on each annual review in terms of appearance and image. One appraisal said "needs to look more professional." I asked them to explain that, and they were uncomfortable, since I was wearing my "dress for success" suit. They told me they wanted me to cut my hair, which I made them put in the appraisal. It is handicapping for a woman to be attractive in a heavily male business. Attractiveness is useful in sales and marketing in the external world, but it can be tremendously jarring in the internal environment with the people you work with on a day-to-day basis. I think that is some of what I face.

In the MIT environment, I considered myself average or below average, but in this work environment, I am smarter than a lot of my supervisors, and it is threatening to them. Being too smart may not be such a good thing.

This consultant left this firm and worked for two more management consulting firms in her specialized area before she made partner about four years later.

Case D: Remained With the Same Firm and Became Principal

First Year Survey. I work for a young firm that is growing rapidly. All of the levels, subordinates, peers, and supervisors are close in age, and we see each other outside of the office. There are only three women consultants out of a professional staff of ninety. I work long hours and am busy, but the work is not intellectually mind-boggling, as when I was in engineering courses in undergraduate school. I received the highest overall rating on my performance review and will be promoted after another six months.

Two-Year Survey. I was promoted to project director (associate) after two and a half years. I did not receive the promotion after one and a half years on the job, but I received a large raise and a large bonus ($10,000), based on my general performance. Also, the fact that new MBAs coming to the firm were making more money than people already there was a factor.

I worry about the ability to bring in business and in this company, this is the only way to become a principal or a partner. My supervisor is a great guy. He has helped me to get the experience I need at this stage of my career, especially the political savvy.

Five-Year Survey. I will be considered for promotion to upper management by next year. However, I need to work on my ability to do marketing—the entrepreneurial side. The consulting job has changed a lot in five years. Initially, what they valued were your analytical skills and everything was very task oriented, but as you progressed, the emphasis shifted to project management, and ultimately sales and marketing.

I have learned a lot in five years and have recently concluded that indeed there are issues in consulting, which are women's issues. As I look around during the past five years, I have seen a number of women come and go. In fact, I am the only senior woman on staff. I think that women who have had non-traditional backgrounds have done better here. Women who are used to dealing in male-oriented or male-dominated situations are doing better. For me it was my undergraduate experiences in engineering.

Some of the things that still concern me as you are reviewed for eventually becoming a partner, is your executive presence or stature. I have not experienced sexual harassment, but I find it a bit difficult to establish credibility. This may be due to the fact that I am young to be a project director. It makes the job a bit more difficult. So during the past year I have modified my behavior a bit and played the game a little more than I used to.

This consultant was promoted to principal a little more than a year later.

Case E: Older Woman With Several Years Business Experience Prior to Sloan School and Another Graduate Degree

First Year Survey. As senior associate on an engagement team, I am responsible for data collection, interpretation and recommendations around the problem solving situation. I accept the general evidence that few people remain in consulting all of their careers. I expect to work for two to five years and then join a corporation. Now, I have a broad range of consulting assignments, so that as I change jobs, I will be able to take on general manager's responsibilities and not have to be a staff specialist. This consulting firm is strongly "up or out." I don't anticipate being one of the "uppers." I don't believe that I am a brilliant conceptual thinker or even given to always recognizing the forest from the trees. These flaws will limit me.

Two-Year Survey. I have been promoted to junior engagement manager, which means that I will have supervisory responsibility for an associate, as well as new tasks having to do with planning of the study, the actual writing of the report, and the relationship with the client. You need three types of skills for the job: (1) ability to problem solve in an analytical fashion, (2) good oral skills, (3) good written skills. I still feel that my writing is my weakest point, and I continue to work at it. It is not that I can't write well, it is just that it takes me too long to do so.

This is the first time I have ever worked for a female supervisor. The woman is slightly older than I, and she has a completely different background (non-technical) from mine. On the whole, I have found this to be an extremely enjoyable experience, not because she is a woman, but because she has the ability to motivate and manage people completely by the carrot and never by the stick. If I could learn to do that as well, that would be one of the best things I could get out of my year with her.

Five-Year Survey. I have been promoted to senior engagement manager and as such, lead the day-to-day operations of problem solving by one or two teams for one or two clients. Success is measured by whether the client accepts your recommendations, implements them, and asks you to work on other substantive issues. I am perceived as an "average" success. I don't feel that what I have accomplished to date really meets these success measures. However, I measure success by whether my upward movement stays even with my peers. I have done so, and frankly surprised myself.

The constraint on my election to partner is that I must show client or clientele development (i.e., not current clients, but potential ones). My co-workers perceive me as good with specialist skills, working too hard, not a superstar, but likely to be elected to partner. If not elected as partner in two years, I am out.

This woman consultant was probably surprised to make partner within one year after the five-year survey. The next case differs from the preceding in that race was a contributing factor to some difficulties in career development, and eventually this minority female left management consulting for a small minority firm.

Case F: Minority Female, Promoted to Principal and Left Industry (Exit)

Two-Year Survey. My title has not changed, but my functional responsibilities have expanded. I am now co-managing a team of ten people. They are all MBAs or in computer science. I average about sixty-five hours a week and in peak times more. I have received increases in salary every six months. People would say you are doing well, your work is good, but you are not aggressive enough. They want you to sell yourself. I was always turned off by people who were busy selling themselves, but it is what the company expects. Even at Sloan, I rarely participated in class. It took me two years to figure out that I was supposed to let them know what I wanted. I was told that I was bright, but that I would not go further by just being bright. Thus, I was initially by-passed in the assignment of management responsibility on a large project that I had designed for the client.

My supervisor's decision on whether to give me management responsibility, I think, was affected by the fact that I was the first minority MBA that he had had any dealings with. I am the only minority female MBA in the company. I don't think that people around me have realized how difficult it is for me to be in that position. Since I am the company's only minority MBA, the company's judgment on future MBAs will be based on me.

Five-Year Survey. After five years with the management consulting firm, I became an officer in a small minority financial and systems design firm. I was promoted to principal before I left the consulting firm, but I had to fight for it. I was the first minority MBA hired by the consulting firm, among the youngest of my peer group, and I had no prior work experience before attending Sloan School. It took me a long time to find out that you had to manipulate people and play games. Although I received big raises, I had to fight two years to be promoted to principal. It was very frustrating. I worked very hard and delivered for the client and was told I was not promoted be-cause I was so much younger (eleven years younger) than the supervisor and that my time would come. When I decided to leave, it created a big corpo-rate uproar over the loss of their only minority consultant. Yet no one asked me why I was leaving.

The experience of these six women consultants is generally repre-sentative of all Sloan entrants, women as well as men, into this indus-try. Individuals with excellent analytical, verbal, and written skills were hired as associate consultants and expected to spend the next two years on a series of very high task-oriented projects. Those who were favorably assessed were promoted to project director, and here the emphasis was on management of people and resources and inter-action with clients who frequently were senior managers. The pro-gression path from this mid-level position is to principal. However, many persons leave the industry between the second and fifth years, either attracted by good offers from the corporate structure or seek-ing a less demanding job—that is, a reduction in travel schedules and a more routine work week of 50-55 hours. Many of the individuals, especially males, who were divorced during the five-year post-Sloan period worked as management consultants. Both men and women in this industry complained about the severe disruption to their per-sonal lives. Thirty-seven percent of the men and the women who accepted jobs in management consulting upon graduation remained in this industry for five years. The exodus was greatest between the initial and the second year. Tables 4–3 through 4–5 show the inter-industry migration of Sloan MBAs over the five-year period.

Of the seventy-two individuals who were employed in management consulting in their initial year, forty of them, or 56 percent, remained in that industry through the second year. If an adjustment is made for persons who did not respond to the second year questionnaire, but according to alumni records were still in the industry, the retention rate is 66 percent for the first two years. Most of those who shifted out of consulting moved to manufacturing and high technology industries. At the same time sixteen individuals, or 29 percent of the fifty-six individuals in management consulting in year two, entered from manufacturing, high technology, and commercial banking as shown in Table 4–3. These tables also show, in addition to retention rates, the exits from and entries into an industry between two periods. The column and row entries designated as "unknown" are balancing items from individuals in the database who may have been unemployed, out of the labor market, students, or non-respondents.

Entrants into management consulting fell into four categories. One group was transfers from the auditing and accounting divisions of the Big Eight accounting firms to the consulting division of these firms. These intra-firm shifts were from the other service industry to management consulting. Several individuals who were highly specialized in computers and software became self-employed consultants. In the third group, some individuals left large bureaucratic workplaces and were employed in small (ten to fifteen professionals), highly specialized consulting firms. Both health services and environmental issues were frequently found in small operations that had been spun off from larger firms. By the fifth year, several women—the fourth category of entrants—had reduced their hours of work to take care of small children. Some were self-employed consultants working out of their homes for several clients, and others had negotiated consulting arrangements with previous employers. Thus, the anomaly of entrants to management consulting after the initial year who received a lower average salary than those who remained reflected both the part-time effort as well as greater volatility of income for the self-employed.

By year five (see Table 4–4), only thirty individuals, or 54 percent of those in the industry in year two, remained. More individuals left management consulting than entered between years two and five.

Table 4-3. Initial vs. Two-Year Industry Distribution of Sloan MBAs.

Industry	Industry Year 2									Total Initial Year
	Mfg.	High Tech	FIRE	Mgt. Consltg.	Public Sector	Other Services	Invest. Bank	Comm. Bank	Unknown	
Manufacturing	55 64%	7	1	2	—	4	—	—	17	86
High Technology	8	21 49%	—	3	—	1	—	—	10	43
Finance, Insurance, Real Estate	—	1	12 48%	2	1	1	—	1	7	25
Management Consulting	8	2	—	40 56%	—	—	—	—	22	72
Public Sector	—	—	—	—	5 83%	1	—	—	—	6
Other Services	4	2	1	2	2	9 26%	—	—	15	35
Investment Banking	—	—	1	—	—	—	2 50%	—	1	4
Commercial Banking	1	—	—	3	1	1	2	16 49%	9	33
Unknown	2	5	—	4	5	4	—	—	5 20%	25
Military	—	—	—	—	1	—	—	—	1	2
Total	78	38	15	56	15	15	4	17	87	

Columns show entry from other industries. Rows show exodus to other industries by year two. Diagonals are retention rates. Total employed Sloan MBAs is 306 for initial year and 244 for second year.

Table 4-4. Two-Year vs. Five-Year Industry Distribution of Sloan MBAs.

Industry	Industry Year 5										Total Second Year
	Mfg.	High Tech	FIRE	Mgt. Consltg.	Public Sector	Other Services	Invest. Bank	Comm. Bank	Unknown	Non-Busn.	
Manufacturing	38 49%	7	3	3	—	5	1	1	18	2	78
High Technology	3	23 60%	—	1	—	—	—	—	11	—	38
Finance, Insurance, Real Estate	—	—	7 47%	1	—	1	—	1	5	—	15
Management Consulting	4	4	—	30 54%	1	4	1	—	12	—	56
Public Sector	—	—	—	1	5 33%	1	—	—	8	—	15
Other Services	1	3	2	1	1	9 43%	—	—	4	—	21
Investment Banking	—	—	—	—	—	—	2 50%	—	2	—	4
Commercial Banking	—	—	—	—	—	—	1	11 65%	5	—	17
Unknown	2	9	3	6	1	6	—	2	58 67%	—	87
Total	48	46	15	43	8	26	5	15	123	2	

Columns show entry from other industries. Rows show exodus to other industries. Diagonals are retention rates. Total for employed Sloans in the second year is 244 and 210 in the fifth year.

| | | | | | Industry Year 5 | | | | | | | Total |
Industry	Mfg.	High Tech	FIRE	Mgt. Consltg.	Public Sector	Other Services	Invest. Bank	Comm. Bank	Unknown	Military	Non-Busn.	Initial Year
Manufacturing	33 38%	11	3	6	1	4	—	1	26	—	1	86
High Technology	4	21 49%	—	2	—	3	—	—	13	—	—	43
Finance, Insurance, Real Estate	—	1	6 26%	2	1	3	—	3	9	—	—	25
Management Consulting	6	8	1	27 37%	1	2	—	—	26	—	1	72
Public Sector	—	—	—	—	2 33%	2	—	—	2	—	—	6
Other Services	3	1	1	3	1	6 17%	2	—	18	—	—	35
Investment Banking	—	—	1	—	—	—	1 25%	—	2	—	—	4
Commercial Banking	1	—	1	1	—	1	2	11 33%	16	—	—	33
Unknown	1	4	2	2	2	5	—	—	9 36%	—	—	25
Military	—	—	—	—	—	—	—	—	—	2 100%	—	2
Total	48	46	15	43	8	26	5	15	121	2	2	

Columns show entry from other industries. Rows show exodus to other industries. Diagonals are retention rates. Total employed Sloan in the initial year is 306 and 210 in the fifth year.

Again, allowing for those who did not respond to the fifth year survey but were known to still be employed in the industry, the retention rate at the end of five years was less than half of those who started initially in the industry. Since most of the part-time women employees (who are not included in these tables) worked in management consulting, both the percentage of total employment and the retention rate in the fifth year was slightly higher.

MANUFACTURING

Initially, 30 percent of the women Sloan MBAs were employed in manufacturing, but by the fifth year the proportion had declined to 18 percent. Like their male Sloan counterparts, these women worked in corporate offices. The experiences of two women who worked on the floor and supervised blue collar workers reveal an aspect of manufacturing rarely encountered by MBAs. These two cases detail the unique experience of women as line managers.

The first woman worked on the plant floor for six months as a first-line supervisor. She was a manager in the Department of Human Resources and had been asked to develop a training package for foremen. With permission from the operations manager, she worked as a foreman for thirty-six men.

> Foremen are looked at as third-class citizens at my company and nothing was being done for them. I had to work as a foreman in order to understand some of the basic issues. The floor is a job shop environment and discipline problems were fairly significant. It was dirty, noisy, heavy equipment and not all that safe. It was tougher for the men than me, because they never had a woman boss before. The shop steward did not know how to talk to me. He couldn't scream at me. He felt he couldn't swear at me. So they were all on their good behavior. The housekeeping improved, the losses dropped, and productivity increased.
>
> I had a lot of problems. It was one of the toughest things I had ever done in my life. The shift started at 7:00 am and when you work overtime, it was put back to 5:00 am. As foreman, you have to get there an hour before the shift starts, in order to get your lines set up and make sure you know where all of the work is. We worked seven days a week for six weeks straight. You are a zombie working those hours. As a result of this, I designed an orientation and training program for college graduates who now start on the floor. We did not have any managers in the high echelon who knew anything about the manufacturing process.

Although this individual was pleased with the consequences of a short tour of duty on the shop floor, it was not routinely a part of her job; one assumes that some of the beneficial effects on discipline and productivity dissipated shortly after her departure.

The second woman was assigned as a first-line supervisor of forty-four blue collar workers in a production area. As a first-line supervisor she kept track of inventories, ran production schedules, coordinated safety features, disciplined workers, hired and fired, and checked quality control. She was the only MBA supervisor, and her peers were engineers. When she left a year later, in her words, "I was a basket case." With her permission, the author has summarized a lengthy taped interview, because it might be beneficial to others. The author also had the unusual opportunity of a field trip to one of the facilities and the opportunity to meet with other first-line supervisors and senior management. The company has been disguised, and the Sloan graduate is referred to as "Nancy."

Nancy had a dual concentration in finance and operations research at the Sloan School. At the age of twenty-three and with little prior work experience, she accepted a job as a team leader in manufacturing, because she was intrigued by the opportunity to work where innovative management techniques were being tested. These experiments were dismantled shortly after she started to work, and the company returned to more traditional styles. Nevertheless, for the next eight months, she supervised a predominantly male blue collar work group on alternating shifts and received an acceptable performance appraisal from three supervisors. They indicated her strengths as the ability to deal with people, openness to new ideas, capacity for hard work, and her major weakness as a technical one, "not knowing when someone 'flim flammed' you on equipment being broken." She was given some training manuals to learn the equipment.

Because she felt isolated, had no one to talk to on the job, and felt that her older male supervisors had very low expectations of women, she asked to be transferred to another facility, closer to home. At the time, she noted that

one of the hardest things in manufacturing that I would tell a woman about, would be to be prepared to have a hard time finding someone to talk to. You don't have the common base to discuss sex, sports, or machinery, the topics of interest to 'macho' blue collar types. There were no young women in my plant and even if I had found someone elsewhere in the company to discuss some of the issues, you may not have the time to do it. You operate in a crisis environment. You feel so alone. The split shift makes it hard to have any routine in your life. My supervisors do not understand why you are in this type of job, and they constantly ask "Why are you here? What are you trying to do?

The request for a transfer after a tenure of less than a year was contrary to company policy. Nancy did not know this at the time. The company arranged the transfer because it was anxious to keep its few women managers. Nancy said: "I was very demanding, very programmed by Sloan to think that you are pretty smart and pretty special. Also, the people I worked with gave me that same impression. 'You are going to be the first woman plant manager.' After the company forced the second facility to accept someone that it had not hired and did not want, and left her alone, the stage was set for failure, loss of esteem, pain, and a short-term illness. From the beginning, she was treated as an outsider by her peers at the second facility.

The transfer to the second facility was approved even though the normal policy of the company was not to allow a transfer at such an early stage. Because of the rapid turnover of newly hired women managers, the company perhaps believed that the transfer might help to retain someone who had the potential to be a plant manager. Nancy was assigned an office physically away from everyone else. She continues her story.

Meanwhile, the only way you could have picked up the information that I needed to know was through interaction with other managers. I spent time with the operators and tried to learn the process. I used to go into the chemical engineer's office and ask him if I could go to school because I did not seem to be getting the information that I needed. 'Oh, no you don't need to go to school; we can teach you everything you need to know right here.' Eventually, I passed the test of technical knowledge and qualified as a supervisor.

I was then threatened by my male colleague, a supervisor who had been there a year and a half ahead of me. He said that no one there liked an outsider and that the operators were giving him feedback that they found me difficult to take. I think that he was threatened by working with a woman on an equal basis. He had worked earlier with another young woman, who had been promoted and he had not. After four months of harassment by this male peer, our problems started to hurt departmental production and one of our co-workers suggested that a third party should come in and try to work things out. Our boss was near retirement, was not a strong leader, and he did not see a problem or understand what was going on. He did not intervene.

It was so hard for me to try to learn the technological aspects of the job in order to know when the workers were sabotaging the equipment. I tried as hard as I could; I got into things and got dirty. Also, the guys I supervised were a very macho group. They joked, laughed, told dirty jokes and talked baseball and football. For someone who was not involved in sports, it was difficult. I tried to deal with them individually, rather than walk in the relief area and say, 'Hey guys, how are you doing?' I did not know how to play the company games. It was not obvious to me, because we did not get together as a management team.

The OD (Organization Development) intervention was not helpful, but I stayed another eight months, which was two years after I had started to work for the company. Afterwards, my plant manager at the first facility said he knew I was having a hard time, and he thought that I would call him. It never occurred to me to call him, because he was a plant manager and three levels above me. I did not want to appear to be a 'crybaby.' I felt there was not a single person I could talk to. I had an emotional collapse as a result of the work environment. I supported myself for one full year in part-time jobs across the country (bookstores, shops, house sitting, etc.), because I could not face the feeling of failure and did not feel I could face family or friends. I took placement counseling and felt extreme apprehension upon accepting a job as a staff planner in another manufacturing company. A year later, I was promoted to senior sales representative and moved to another geographic area.

A senior official from my first job contacted me during my 'burn-out' year and asked me to return to the first plant to talk with him, some of my former colleagues, and an organizational development specialist. The OD person said that I had committed 'corporate suicide,' but that I should try to find employment at another manufacturing company where managers are strictly white collar workers. My former peers said that they had worked with maybe six people who had followed after me, and that I undoubtedly was the best. Looking back on this experience, I feel that being female was and still is the toughest adjustment towards a management career.

In both of the cases discussed above, the women worked as first-line supervisors. The first-line supervisors, the "men in the middle," between management and the work force in many companies, have been promoted from the ranks, and in others are management trainees who are recent college graduates. It has not been a position where women have been especially welcomed. The job is difficult and complicated and peer support is necessary. Technical or mechanical difficulties have been experienced by female first-line supervisors in other manufacturing concerns,[8] but the assignment of an MBA to a work unit where all of the first-line supervisors were engineers was a major mistake. The company learned how better to handle young women first-line supervisors. It is likely that few women MBAs will experience such difficulties in the future, because they will seek the white collar jobs if they work in manufacturing. The various forms of the automated factory, with its special repair and maintenance teams, will lessen the need to be so knowledgeable about the equipment.

The retention rate for Sloan MBAs in manufacturing was 64 percent in year two. Of the eighty-six individuals who had accepted jobs in manufacturing in the initial year, fifty-five remained in that industry at the second year. (See Table 4-3.) The largest number of new entrants into manufacturing at year two was from management consulting and the high technology industries. By the fifth year, one-half of those in this industry in year two remained. Men were more inclined to migrate into manufacturing, and women to move away from manufacturing to other services and high technology. Only one-third of the women who started in manufacturing remained there at the end of five years, as compared with about two-fifths of the men. The retention rates, exodus from, and entry into the various industry sectors over a five-year period reveals considerable mobility for the Sloan graduates who accepted jobs immediately upon graduation. The fact that only 38 percent of those who started out in the manufacturing sector in the initial year remained in this industry means considerable "churning about" by Sloan MBAs. However, 59 percent remaining after two years, 53 percent between the second and fifth years, and 42 percent at the end of five years shows greater stability in what is usually described as the manufacturing sector (manufacturing including high technology).

RETENTION RATES FOR REMAINING INDUSTRIES

The retention rate (individuals working in an industry as a percent of those similarly employed in some base period) is one measure of mobility. These mobility patterns varied across industries, as indicated in Table 4-6. During the first two years, the overall retention rate of individuals who remained in their industry of initial employ-

Table 4-6. Retention Rates of Sloan MBAs in Major Industries.

Industry	Percent		
	Second/Initial	Five/Second	Five/Initial
Manufacturing[a]	59	53	42
Management Consulting	56	54	37
Financial Services[b]	48	56	30
Other Services	26	43	17
Total	53	51	35

a. Combined manufacturing and high technology.
b. Combined finance, insurance and real estate, investment and commercial banking.

ment was 53 percent. With the exception of the other services category, which is the industry category with the lowest private sector pay, all of the larger, other industrial sectors experienced comparable retention rates. The inter-industry shifts between the second and the fifth years yielded an overall retention rate of 51 percent. The improvement in the retention rate of other services to 43 percent by the fifth year reflects the movement of women out of management consulting and manufacturing into health, education, and welfare services.

At the same time, men left management consulting for the manufacturing and high technology industries. The women who moved to other industries, where salaries were lower, rationalized their choices based on jobs that they perceived to be more socially useful. These women frequently discussed that utilizing their managerial skills in workplaces (schools, hospitals, etc.) in need of better management practices was very rewarding. The overall retention rate for all industries between the initial and fifth year was 35 percent. Making adjustments for non-response in the fifth year, it is fairly certain that about three-fifths of the Sloan MBAs left their industry of initial employment by the fifth year after graduation. This proportion may have been normal for new MBAs who were positioning themselves for fast track careers and who were not particularly loyal to any employer.

In addition to these inter-industry exits and entrances, the promotions, functions, and job changes, intra-industry, as described in the preceding chapter defined a young managerial population effectively using various mobility options to achieve success in their careers. Although the majority of the shifts were upward mobility changes, lateral and occasionally, downward mobility also occurred.

CONCLUSION

Several of the narratives in this chapter spoke of learning to play the "game." In Schein's description of the dimensions of the early career playing, the "game" might include overcoming the insecurity of inexperience, deciphering the culture of the organization, learning to get along with the boss, accepting subordinate status, learning from the initiation rites and other rituals associated with being a novice, accepting responsibility, and developing initiative and a realistic level of aggressiveness within the limits of the job.[9] If Sloan MBAs had worked prior to matriculation in the graduate management program, they were somewhat knowledgeable about the world of work and started their postgraduate careers without too much difficulty.

The transformation from full-time student to full-time worker was more problematic for those who had limited work experience, about one-third of the Sloan MBAs. At the end of two years they were more likely to complain of red tape, incompetent supervisors, and "politicking." But by the fifth year most of the Sloan MBAs had matured and had learned to get along with peers, subordinates, and supervisors. For both women and minorities the adjustments were not as easy. Chapter 5 discusses the additional costs that women paid to reach middle management. At the end of five years, minority Sloan MBAs lagged behind their counterparts, both other Sloan MBAs and their peers at work, in achieving their career objectives.

NOTES

1. U.S. Office of Management and Budget, *Standard Industrial Classification Manual* (Washington, D.C.: U.S. Government Printing Office, 1972). The SIC is a classification structure, by level detail, of the primary products or activities of industries.

2. High technology industries include electronic computing equipment (SIC 3573), electronic components (SIC 3674), measuring and controlling instruments (SIC 3811), research and development laboratories (SIC 7391), engi-

neering services (SIC 891), computer software, and other computer related services (SIC 737).

3. Lee Berton, "Touche Ross and Co. Buys Braxton, Inc.," *The Wall Street Journal*, 4 December 1984.

4. Elizabeth M. Fowler, "Consulting Marked By Changes." *The New York Times*, 7 July 1987.

5. Myra H. Strober, "The MBA: Same Passport to Success for Women and Men?" in P.A. Wallace, ed., *Women in the Workplace* (Boston: Auburn House Publishing Co., 1982), pp. 25–44.

6. Chester C. Levine, "Miscellaneous Business Services: Little Known But Growing Fast," *Occupational Outlook Quarterly* 29 (Summer 1985): 20-5.

7. "The Consulting Springboard," *Business Week*, 17 August 1981.

8. Henry Hale and Homi Patel, *Female First Line Supervisors: Prescriptions, Problems, and Performance*, Master's thesis, Sloan School at MIT, June 1979.

9. Edgar H. Schein, *Career Dynamics: Matching Individual and Organizational Needs* (Reading, Mass.: Addison-Wesley Publishing Co., 1978), pp. 41–42.

5 COMPENSATION
Money Isn't Everything

MBAs, especially the graduates of the leading business schools are well-paid professionals who may earn salaries that are at least 50 percent higher than those of average families in the United States. In 1984, median earnings of families with a householder working full-time/full year was $35,788, and salaries of those employed as executives, administrators, and managers was $42,996.[1] The beginning salary of graduates from the Sloan School in that year averaged $39,000, and the fifth year salaries of the Sloan School sample for this text was an average of $49,109, both in current dollars.[2] Most of the research on the occupational achievement of MBAs has focused on beginning salaries. This chapter will examine the structure of MBA salaries during the five-year period after graduation and will discuss salary differences between male and female MBAs. Comparisons between minority MBAs and non-minority MBAs are included in Chapter 6.

The principal finding on salary is that there were no significant differences between the fifth year salaries of male and female MBAs who worked full time. Yet female MBAs paid a higher psychic cost for their occupational success. Job-related stress was significantly higher for women in both year two and year five. In addition, nine women opted for part-time work schedules to care for small children, and not one male made such arrangements. Some of the complexities of cross-gender mentor/protege relationships and their significance for women managers in predominately male work settings are also examined.

Although compensation includes base pay, incentives (bonuses), stock options, and a variety of other benefits, the data from this research are based on salary; where bonuses were reported, salary and bonuses were aggregated. The initial year and two-year salaries, by industry of employment, are discussed prior to a more detailed analysis of fifth year salaries for MBAs. Also, salaries of Sloan MBAs are compared with graduates from other management schools. Economists focus mainly on earnings as the measure of success in an occupation or career. Expected lifetime earnings determine the type of investment by individuals in human capital. For example, individuals who have a graduate degree in management (the MBA) expect and generally receive a high return on their investment. The MBA is perceived as a productivity enhancing credential, and when it is associated with additional on-the-job-training, experience/earnings profiles are sharply raised. In a labor market free of barriers and absent of discrimination, salary is regarded as the best reward for satisfactory job performance.[3]

Non-pecuniary rewards are also important in the job/salary match for the individual, but the focus here is on salary, which can be easily aggregated and adjusted for inflation. Because of a significant escalation in nominal MBA salaries during the latter part of the 1970s, and double-digit inflation in the economy, salaries for the 1975–84 period are given in 1983 constant dollars, using the Consumer Price Index (CPI). Average, annual beginning salaries of MBAs with technical undergraduate degrees and limited work experience increased from $16,000 in 1975 to $30,000 by 1984. Nominal salaries of Sloan School MBAs with technical backgrounds and one year or less of full-time work experience also rose from $18,000 to $36,000 during this period.[4]

A sizeable psychosocial literature on motivation and reward systems exists,[5] but the study has investigated the impact of only a number of key economic variables on fifth-year salaries such as industry of employment, prior work experience, hours, and job-related travel. Pfeffer found that socioeconomic origins were one of the important predictor variables for current salaries of male MBAs.[6] The economic paradigm here treats both motivation and personal characteristics as givens. Finally, we believe that the salaries reported here are more precise than in some of the published research. A separate questionnaire was sent out initially, plus two and five years after commencement. There was little retrospective effort to recall the salary received several years in the past. Thus, data were collected over a ten-year period beginning with the initial salary of the class of 1975 and ending in 1984, with the five-year reports from the class of 1979.

INITIAL YEAR SALARIES

Initial year salaries are negotiated between Sloan School students in their last year of the Master's Program and prospective employers who recruit on campus. About one-quarter of the Sloan MBAs had enrolled in the twelve-month Accelerated Master's Program (AMP) and looked for jobs in their spring term. The AMPs were slightly older and had more work experience. Beginning salaries for the MBAs reflect several factors such as functional skills, prior work experience, education, age, geographic location, and whatever innate characteristics an employer perceived to be embodied in an individual. Based on the analysis, it appears that prior work experience was a plus for men but not necessarily for women. Many of the women who entered Sloan School in the mid-1970s had worked in the public sector or for nonprofit agencies, and private sector employers discounted this experience. Men either had served as military officers or had worked as engineers or as other professionals and were rewarded for these experiences. At the same time, women may have received an initial bonus because the 1970s was an era of aggressive recruiting of women managers into non-traditional jobs. It was cheaper to buy newly credentialed female MBAs than to invest heavily in the training and retreading of women already employed in staff or other professional jobs. Several men who had technical degrees and five years of work experience received an additional bonus when they accepted an offer.

Initial year salaries for Sloan MBAs averaged $32,840, with women earning $31,910 and men $33,350. This difference of $1,440 was not statistically significant—see Figure 5-1. The year of graduation had an impact on the initial year salaries for males but not for females. In 1979, men received approximately $4,000 more than women. Since the initial salaries for men and women in the preceding four years were about the same, the only explanation for this devia-

Figure 5-1. Salaries of Sloan MBAs by Period (*1983 constant dollars*).

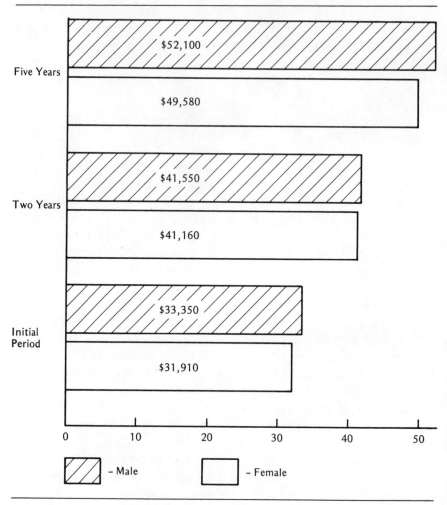

tion seems to be industry related, in that although women accepted jobs in manufacturing, more accepted positions in personnel and employee relations departments than in previous years. No males in the class of 1979 worked in these positions. Our research shows one of the major determinants of salary to be industry of employment. Management consulting employed 24 percent of the Sloan MBAs and paid them the second highest annual beginning salary of $36,000. In the preceding chapter, management consulting was noted as the growth industry for MBAs in the late 1970s. The lowest annual sal-

Table 5-1. Salary by Industry of Employment for Sloan MBAs
(*in thousands, 1983 constant dollars*).

Industry	Initial Year	Second Year	Fifth Year
Manufacturing	32.4	40.6	49.6
High Technology	33.7	40.2	46.7
Finance, Insurance, Real Estate	32.5	49.2	74.3
Management Consulting	36.1	45.5	54.6
Public Sector	25.7	34.6	34.4
Other Services	29.4	35.9	43.5
Investment Banking	39.9	50.2	89.1
Commercial Banking	31.1	36.2	44.8
Male	33.35	41.55	52.10
Female	31.91	41.16	49.58
Total	32.84	41.40	51.18

ary of $25,660, which was only 78 percent of the overall class average, was received by the very few Sloan School MBAs who accepted jobs in the public sector. The salary rankings of the eight industries where Sloan MBAs worked remained approximately the same throughout the five-year period. See Table 5-1.

Manufacturing employed one-third of the Sloan MBAs in the initial year, and the average salary of $32,400 placed it fourth highest of the eight industries. By the fifth year, manufacturing employed a quarter of the Sloan MBAs at an average salary of $49,620, and it remained the fourth highest paying industry. Investment banking was the highest paying industry throughout the period, with an initial salary of $39,950 and a five-year salary of $89,100.

According to a report in *Business Week*, career opportunities in investment banking exploded in the late 1970s. By 1987, more than 30 percent of the Harvard MBA class went into investment banking, at median starting salaries of $50,000. Both Stanford and Wharton each saw 22 percent of their 1986 class go into investment banking.[7] Although less than 3 percent of the Sloan School MBAs were employed in investment banking during the 1975-79 period, by 1985, 10 percent of the class started in investment banking at a salary of $44,100 (not adjusted for inflation). The Sloan MBAs in this study worked in the mergers and acquisitions department of investment banks. One respondent explained that newly hired MBAs were recruited based on their potential to perform above the entry level. Satisfactory performance meant that entry level base salaries would be doubled by the end of two years, and doubled again before the fifth year. In addition to the increases in base salary, employees in investment banks also received very large bonuses.

Initial salaries by functional area of concentration at the Sloan School showed that four areas—finance, international management, planning, and control and marketing; and organizational studies—paid salaries above the $32,840 initial year average. However, the data on organizational studies is skewed by the fact that during the 1970s, an area subgroup of what is now labeled Management of Technology was domiciled in the Organizational Studies unit at the Sloan School. These individuals tended to be experienced engineers who returned to good-paying jobs as managers.

SALARY INCREASES BETWEEN THE INITIAL AND SECOND YEARS

Almost 60 percent of the respondents to the second year survey indicated that they had received salary increases. Salary increases between the initial and second year differed for men and women and by industry. Women MBAs received slightly higher salary increases of $9,400, as compared with $8,430 for men. (See Table 5-2.) In the three industries with the heaviest concentration of individuals, men received slightly higher salary increases. In manufacturing and high technology, the salary increases were higher for men and were approximately the same as for women in management consulting. The highest salary increases overall were in the financial services and investment banking industries. The lowest salary increases were received in commercial banking and may reflect the fact that even MBAs are typically placed in a twelve to eighteen month training program before they become lending officers.

Nearly three-fourths of the salary increases were derived from promotions within the same company. It is not easy to explain why women did better than men in salary increases during their first two years on the job. This period of 1977–81 may have been a time when private employers rapidly promoted extremely capable women.

Table 5-2. Salary Increase Between Initial Year and Year Two by Sex and Industry (*in thousands, 1983 constant dollars*).

Industry	Salary Increase/Women	Salary Increase/Men	Salary Increase/Total
Manufacturing	5.99	7.73	7.23
High Technology	6.23	7.70	7.15
Finance, Insurance, Real Estate	24.40	13.45	17.83
Management Consulting	11.16	11.57	11.41
Public Sector	18.68	0.35	5.99
Other Services	7.44	6.49	7.02
Investment Banking	20.56	14.77	17.67
Commercial Banking	4.48	3.27	3.94
Total Average Increase	9.40	8.43	8.79

One respondent reported that she had three promotions within a short period, and had requested no further promotions until she had learned all the aspects of her greatly expanded job description. She indicated that her company was anxious to have several women in highly visible, line manager jobs and were accelerating the pace for those perceived to be outstanding performers. Some employers may have discounted the prior work experience of the women when they were hired, and once they had an opportunity to evaluate their performance rewarded them accordingly. A much smaller proportion of women than men changed employers during this two-year period, so the higher salary increases might have included some loyalty bonus. These salary increases contributed to a two-year salary with little difference between men and women. This happy state of higher salary increases for women was reversed during the last three years of the five-year period.

SECOND YEAR SALARIES

Second year salaries for Sloan MBAs averaged $41,400, a 26 percent increase over beginning salaries. As shown in Table 5-1, women averaged $41,160 and men $41,550 with salary increases for women slightly ahead. Men received somewhat higher wages than women in manufacturing, high technology, and management consulting. The salary of women exceeded that of males in financial services, the public sector, other services, and commercial banking. All of the second group of industries, with the exception of financial services, had salaries below the overall two-year average of $41,410. Investment banking paid women and men essentially the same salary.

Although in the second year the industry mix for men and women was comparable to ratios that had prevailed in the initial year, women had begun shifting into other services, especially health and education, and men into manufacturing and high technology. In Table 4-1 in Chapter 4 10 percent of the Sloan women worked in other services in the initial years and 21 percent by the fifth year. Forty-three percent of the Sloan men worked in the combined manufacturing and high technology industries in the initial year and 50 percent in the fifth year.

SALARY INCREASES BETWEEN SECOND AND FIFTH YEAR

By the fifth year of postgraduate work experience, over 80 percent of the Sloan MBAs had been promoted one or more times since year two. As indicated in Chapter 3, many had changed their functions along with their employers. During this period, their salaries increased on the average by $10,160 (adjusted for inflation), and men averaged $11,220 as compared with $8,280 for women. (See Table 5-3.) The largest salary increases for both groups were in the financial services and investment banking industries. Salary increases for men were higher than for women in all industries except high technology and investment banking. The $3,000 difference in salary increase in high technology perhaps is attributable to the role of the entrepreneur. By the fifth year, about 15 percent of Sloan male MBAs were entrepreneurs, mostly in high technology. They took significant reductions in salary in order to start new ventures. Their expected long-term monetary return would more than compensate for short-term nominal salary reductions.

The $25,000 difference in investment banking salary increase may reflect the small numbers employed, rather than any useful information about this industry. The flow of individuals between industries

Table 5-3. Salary Increase Between Year Two and Year Five by Sex and Industry (*in thousands, 1983 constant dollars*).

Industry	Salary Increase/Women	Salary Increase/Men	Salary Increase/Total
Manufacturing	6.24	7.80	7.36
High Technology	8.25	4.98	6.14
Finance, Insurance, Real Estate	25.28	28.64	28.03
Management Consulting	6.84	9.95	8.99
Public Sector	-3.55	4.59	1.87
Other Services	6.28	11.77	8.11
Investment Banking	67.00	41.72	46.77
Commercial Banking	7.09	10.64	8.70
Total Average Increase	8.28	11.22	10.16

was a key factor in salary increases. Men who moved to other industries received a larger salary increase, $14,820, but women were severely penalized when they moved to other industries, receiving only a $4,000 salary increase. Women left the better paying management consulting jobs for opportunities in the much lower paying health and educational organizations (other services). Several noted that they traded off between the corporate sector and the helping and nurturing jobs. Essentially, they rationalized, they were utilizing their managerial skills in workplaces sorely in need of these techniques. Sometimes the shift to jobs in health management or educational administration permitted them to add more flexibility and more order to their personal lives, especially if they had children. Also, by year five, more women had married and were relocating to be with spouse/partners. Nevertheless, the whopping $10,820 differential when women moved to other industries was a heavy price to pay.

FIFTH YEAR SALARIES

Fifth year salaries will be examined by industry of employment and by sex. Through regression analysis, variables were identified which were important determinants of fifth year salaries. In constant dollars, salaries in year five had increased 56 percent and 24 percent over the five years and during the last three years of the period, respectively. Male salaries averaged $52,100 and female salaries were 95 percent of that amount, or $49,580. Both men and women had their salaries increased by about 34 percent over the five-year period, but salaries of minorities increased only by 29 percent.

REGRESSION ANALYSIS FOR FIFTH YEAR COMPENSATION

To test the null hypothesis—that, all other things being equal, there were no significant differences in the fifth year compensation of male and female MBAs—a regression analysis was performed. One hundred and seventy-nine individuals (sixty-four women and one hundred and fifteen men, all full-time employees) who responded in both the initial and the fifth year was the group used for the regression analysis. We identified a series of independent variables for their explanatory impact on the dependent variable, fifth year annual compensation (SABU5). A large number of potential explanatory variables were tested (t-tests at the 10 percent level), and eleven independent variables were selected. Prior working experience, hours worked per week, mentors, travel time, and industry where employed affected fifth year compensation. Variables are defined in Table 5–4.

The six industry variables can be viewed as a single industry factor. In a separate regression which excluded the six industry variables, the adjusted R^2 was 0.098, as compared with 0.370 for the regression in which all eleven independent variables were included. The F-statistic, which shows that industry of employment had a significant effect on MBA fifth year compensation (SABU5), is 10.75 which is significant beyond the 0.01 level. Among variables tested and found not to have a significant impact on MBA compensation were: race, discontinuous labor force participation, technical undergraduate degree, and with the exception of finance, concentration while at the Sloan School. The finance, insurance, real estate (FIRE) industry variable picked up the impact of MBA concentration in finance, and the latter was not included as one of the independent variables in the regression analysis. Since a large proportion of Sloan students concen-

Table 5-4. Definition of Variables for Regression Analysis.

SABU5	= MBA Compensation in the fifth year (dependent variable).
HOUR	= Number of hours worked per week.
EXP	= Full-time working experience in years prior to the MBA program.
TRAV5	= Travel time over 25% (= 1, otherwise = 0).[a]
FIRE	= Employed by an investment bank, finance, insurance or real estate companies, but exclude commercial banking (= 1, otherwise = 0).[b]
MANU	= Employed by manufacturing industries, excluding high tech industries (= 1, otherwise = 0).
HITEC	= Employed by high-tech industries (= 1, otherwise = 0).
MCON	= Employed by management consulting companies (= 1, otherwise = 0).
PBUS	= Employed by public sector and non-profit organizations (= 1, otherwise = 0).
CBNK	= Employed by commercial banks (= 1, otherwise = 0).
PMENTOR	= Positive mentor relationship (= 1, otherwise = 0).[c]
NMENTOR	= Negative mentor relationship (= 1, otherwise = 0).[c]

a. In the questionnaire, subjects were asked what percentage of the time their jobs required them to travel and their answers were grouped into six categories; none, up to 10 percent, between 11 percent and 25 percent, between 26 percent and 60 percent, over 60 percent and varies with project. Only the last three categories were significant and after appropriate tests, a dummy variable combining them was used.

b. Commercial banking is excluded from FIRE because of differences in the nature of the job. This results in significant differences in working hours and compensation levels (t-test significance beyond the 0.01 level).

c. 0 = had no mentor.

trate in finance (38 percent of the sample) and are employed in the finance, insurance, and real estate industry, this industry variable reflects this relationship. Also, financial specialists at the end of five years were well represented in manufacturing, high technology, and the management consulting industries.

Of the 179 observations in the sample, 13 were dropped due to missing value for some of the independent variables. The number of observations for the regression analysis was 166 individuals (62 women and 104 men). The regression results of these variables on MBA compensation are shown in Table 5-5. Work experience, sig-

Table 5-5. Regression Results of MBA Fifth Year Compensation.

Variables	Mean (Standard Deviation)	Coefficient (T-Statistic)
Constant	—	24.2*** (2.60)
HOUR	52.27 (9.11)	0.211 (1.37)
EXP	3.35 (3.76)	1.17*** (3.09)
TRAV	0.247 (0.433)	8.15** (2.48)
NMENTR	0.38 (1.69)	-4.67* (-1.96)
PMENTR	0.76 (1.67)	4.95** (2.07)
FIRE	0.102 (0.304)	42.4*** (7.36)
MANU	0.259 (0.439)	8.76* (1.89)
HITEC	0.199 (0.400)	5.39 (1.13)
MCON	0.175 (0.381)	15.4*** (13.07)
PUBS	0.042 (0.202)	-10.1 (-1.31)
CBNK	0.084 (0.279)	8.30 (1.38)
SEX	0.373 (0.485)	-0.51 (-0.18)
SABU5	53.7 (21.74)	— —
R^2	—	0.416
$\bar{R}^2$	—	0.370
SEE	—	17.3
Number of observations[a]	—	166

a. Excluding part-time workers, students, military personnel, and non-business employees.

　　*Significant at 10 percent level.
　　**Significant at 5 percent level.
　　***Significant at 1 percent level.

nificant travel time, mentors, and industry of employment (especially FIRE and management consulting) have significant impact on the fifth year compensation. The management consulting coefficient indicates that the effect on MBA compensation is $15,400. However, there are correlations between the eleven dependent variables. For example, Sloan MBAs employed in investment banking tend to work long hours, 55.8 hours per week on the average as compared to the average of 51.7 hours per week for the entire sample. Management consultants travel extensively and thus tend to report relatively long hours. The highly demanding industries such as investment banking and management consulting paid a significantly higher salary. These characteristics of employers (long hours and extensive travel) may pose multicollinearity problems to the regression results. As expected, working in the public sector has a negative (but not significant) impact on the level of compensation.

The significance of sex on MBA fifth year compensation was tested by including a dummy variable representing sex. The sex variable, with a coefficient of -0.51 and a t-statistic of only -0.18, had almost no effect on MBA compensation—that is, after considering the differences in industry of employment, travel time, mentor relationship, prior working experience, and number of hours worked per week, Sloan female MBAs received pay equal to Sloan male MBAs. Five years after graduation from the Sloan School, the difference between the female MBA salary of $51,000 and the male MBAs salary of $53,700 is apparently accounted for by factors other than sex. We have reason to doubt that female and male MBAs are treated the same at work, even if no significant statistical differences are revealed in the dollar amount of compensation. As discussed below, women reported significantly more job-related stress even in the fifth year, and a much higher percentage of women (71 percent) than men (41 percent) indicated that they had to modify their behavior in order to fit into the organization.

The differences in fifth year compensation between male and female MBAs were tested with the eleven variables and the regression model discussed above.* This model was also run separately for the male and female respondents in the sample and these separate regressions revealed some surprises. Some independent variables were significant for males, but not for females. (See Table 5-6.) Work expe-

---

*Regressing the logarithm of the dependent variable (fifth-year compensation in 1983 constant dollars) on the same independent variables yields similar results.

Table 5-6. Structure of Male and Female MBA Compensation.

Variables	Male MBAs Coefficients (T-Statistic)	Female MBAs Coefficients (T-Statistic)
Constant	30.0** (2.54)	4.59 (0.30)
HOUR	0.055 (0.30)	0.689*** (2.49)
EXP	1.60*** (3.07)	0.276 (0.522)
TRAV	15.0*** (3.53)	−6.01 (−1.22)
NMENTR	−8.27** (−2.33)	−2.53 (−0.87)
PMENTR	8.83** (2.49)	2.12 (0.74)
FIRE	39.5*** (4.85)	50.3*** (6.38)
MANU	4.96 (0.70)	7.14 (1.21)
HITEC	2.55 (0.35)	6.97 (1.29)
MCON	13.5* (1.80)	19.4*** (3.14)
PUBS	−14.8 (−1.31)	4.94 (0.51)
CBNK	11.1 (1.18)	4.92 (0.73)
SABU5	53.7	51.0
R^2	0.456	0.546
$\overline{R}^2$	0.391	0.447
SEE	18.32	13.7
Number of observations[a]	104	62

a. Excluding part-time workers, students, military personnel, and non-business employees.

*Significant at 10 percent level.

**Significant at 5 percent level.

***Significant at 1 percent level.

rience prior to receiving the MBA was significant in the regression results on aggregate MBA fifth year compensation ($1,170), but in the disaggregated male and female regressions, this is a significant variable only for men and not for women. For male MBAs, prior work experience, travel, employment in management consulting and financial services, and the presence of a mentor had a significant impact on compensation. However, except for financial services and management consulting, the other variables are not significant for women. Hours worked per week is significant for women but not for men; this may be due to the fact that the travel variable may pick up the effect of the number of hours worked in the males' regression. After dropping the travel variable out of the male regression, the hours variable is still not significant. Closer examination of the data shows that women worked more hours than men in four out of seven industries, especially manufacturing industries.

Although there are differences in the determinants of compensation between male and female MBAs, these differences are not statistically significant. At the 5 percent significance level, as shown by covariance analysis, the hypothesis cannot be rejected that the overall structure of MBAs compensation is the same for men and women. Structure differences are defined here as the extent to which the eleven variables explain the variances of fifth year compensation (SABU5). The hypothesis also cannot be rejected that the overall structure, slope vectors, and intercepts of the fifth year MBA compensation are the same between men and women. Given the relatively high but not significant F-statistics, there is reason to believe that there is different treatment in work that is not reflected in significant differences in the dollar amount of compensation. The analysis of the mentoring relationship that follows supports this conclusion. Although female Sloan MBAs are more likely to report receiving more mentoring than do males, these relationships did not have a significant impact on their compensation levels.

Sloan MBAs fared well during the first five years of post-management school experience. Compensation for both men and women increased by about 56 percent over the five-year period, with the greatest increases in financial services (including investment banking), followed by manufacturing and management consulting. In terms of their economic achievement, female MBAs had started their careers receiving equal pay and after five years were not lagging behind males. Since female MBAs were represented in all of the industries where the industry of employment variable was a significant determinant of earnings, their monetary gains were comparable to the male MBAs. Analysis of variance shows an insignificant difference between fifth year salaries of men and women.

PERSONAL CHARACTERISTICS
OF SLOAN MBAs

To examine the higher psychic costs which female MBAs appear to have paid for their occupational success, an attempt was made to determine the relationship, if any, between their personal characteristics and their careers. The initial profile for Sloan MBAs in Chapter 3 shows that they were young (a mean age of 26.7 years at graduation), white individuals, 35 percent of whom were women. The research design excluded foreign students from the Sloan School sample. Although two out of five were married, very few had children. They had attended quality undergraduate institutions and had 3.2 years of full-time work experience before enrolling at the Sloan School. Both men and women had accepted good-paying jobs, nearly all in the private sector. There were no questions on the survey instruments on socioeconomic status, but in conversations with many of the women, the author concluded that they had come from affluent families. Several saw their very successful fathers as role models.

At the time of the second-year follow-up survey, nearly half of the Sloan MBAs had married; 6 percent were divorced, and 10 percent had children. In their response to a question on integrating their work and non-work activities, 55 percent reported some problems, with a much higher percentage of women (73 percent) responding than men (46 percent). A higher percentage of women MBAs (56 percent) than men (37 percent) noted that the job affected their personal lives, and a smaller proportion of women (52 percent) than men (70 percent) felt that their personal lives had no effect on their jobs. At the end of two years, when more than half of the Sloan MBAs were exceedingly satisfied on their jobs and at least two-thirds were more than satisfied with their performance appraisals, women were more negatively affected than men on some of the psychosocial variables. (See Table 3-2 in Chapter 3.) Job-related stress was significantly higher for them at both year two and year five. Contributing to the job-related stress for women was the fact that after five years they still experienced significant job credibility problems. They had modified their behavior in order to fit into their organizations and tried to cope in several ways. Stress issues will be discussed later in this chapter.

After five years, 61 percent of the Sloan MBAs, about the same percentage for men and women, were married; however, more than half did not have children. The conflict between their careers and their personal lives remained a problem for some, with about 30 percent reporting "a lot" of interference between their jobs and personal lives, and only slightly more than half reporting that they were satisfied with the balance between their professional and personal lives. Both men and women expressed a wish to devote more time to their families, athletic activities, a social life, hobbies. On average, they spent about ten hours per month on non-work related activities outside of the home (jogging, skiing, sailing, tennis). All of the trend data are reported in tables in Chapter 3 and Appendix A.

Women made more adjustments than did men in terms of work schedules and child care arrangements. All of the part-time workers at year five (4 percent of all respondents) were women. Of the nine women part-time employees in the fifth year, five devoted their non-market time to taking care of small children. Three were self-employed on a part-time basis, as they made critical transitions in their careers, and one had recently relocated with a spouse and had some difficulty finding a job comparable to her previous one. Three of the part-time working mothers had two children.

One Sloan female, a part-time working mother with two children, explains why she decided to return to full-time employment:

> With a second child, I decided to work at home on a part-time basis, but found it frustrating. My colleagues at work simply did not think of me as a part of their decision-making team, even though I did the equivalent of three full days a week. I found that working in an adjunct position did not satisfy my career.
>
> I also discovered when I worked at home how difficult it was to try to juggle family and career to the extent that I would like to do it. You have to cut back on either family or career commitment because together they take more than twenty-four hours. I am leary of returning to a full-time job, even though I have full-time child care. I looked for something where I did not have to travel and where I would be assured of doing only forty hours a week.

> We are a dual career family, and have had many arguments at home about baby sitting responsibilities. However, we are able to shift schedules, and if need be, my husband can take the children to the office with him. He chose his firm because most of the people are family-oriented. Without my husband's support, I could not consider a full-time job.

This case is typical of the part-time working mothers in the Sloan School study. They have usually been able to negotiate a part-time consulting arrangement with their employers. They expected to return to full-time employment once their children were older, but they saw a low probability of returning to fast track positions. They knew that they would be replaced by members of the baby boom generation who were as smart, ambitious, and energetic as themselves. Almost all Sloan women were married to men who had advanced further in their careers.

All individuals with children were asked about child care arrangements, and 70 percent of the males indicated that a non-working spouse handled child care. Female MBAs relied mostly on sitters and day care arrangements. Several reported that they had live-in housekeepers. Even women without children identified their ability to cope with child care arrangements as a future problem and a prospective source of conflict with their careers. Child care is one of the areas where private sector employers have not readily accommodated the special needs of married, women managers. To some extent, employers may believe that well-paid female managers should treat child care as a purely personal purchase of a service from appropriate vendors and some support may be given to non-managerial, clerical, single parents. In 1986 only 2 percent, or 25,000 business and government employers, sponsored day care centers for their workers' children.[8]

STRESS

If mentoring is considered a productivity-enhancing component of human capital, job-related stress may be deterimental to productivity. Managerial stress has been defined by Ivancevich and Matteson as an internal response to a disruptive external agent, the stressor.[9] Among the sources of stress from the work environment identified in this study are work overload, role ambiguity, non-supportive supervisors, loss of discretionary responsibility, inadequacy in the job, and organizational issues. Stress is linked to psychological problems such as depression, anxiety, apathy, psychosomatic illnesses, and to physiological changes such as elevated heart rates, blood pressures, and cholesterol levels. In Chapter 3 a significant difference was reported in the level of stress for male and female Sloan MBAs. Until recently, women were conspicuously absent from studies on managerial stress. The stress at work literature was developed at first from studies of blue-collar workers. Studies of stress for managers were more recent, and the population was all male.

After updating statistics[10] derived from the Sloan School five-year surveys, the study found that a larger percentage of males reported that they did not experience job-related stress—28 percent, as compared with 14 percent for women. Thus, the dual burden of performing in a managerial capacity and frequently as the single or one of few high-ranking women in a predominately male work setting continues to be stressful, even after five years. Women may have additional non-work pressures that stem from commitments to family concerns. However, both men and women have indicated that the overwhelming proportion of their stress is caused by the work environment, not activities in their personal lives. Some indirect indications of stress were included in inquiries about balance of work and home life, job security, work relationships, dual career concerns, potential sources of support, and changes in job or personal life.

Even after they have gained considerable work experience, women managers remain at greater risk than male managers in experiencing high levels of stress. Why? Harlan and Weiss hypothesize that the increased presence of able women managers will pose new threats and new problems. They state that the level of resistance by male managers to the first women managers in a company will be high, but will decrease as the percentage of women managers rises to approximately 10–15 percent. Beyond this point, the level of resistance rises again as male managers perceive a threat- and the level of resistance intensifies.[11]

Of the Sloan graduates who reported stress, 43 percent of the women and 51 percent of the men indicated that stress had hurt their job performance. The three most frequently mentioned stressors for women were inadequacy in the job; role ambiguity; and work overload: The three stressors most frequently mentioned for men were role ambiguity, work overload, and organizational issues. With the exception of the stressor of non-supportive supervisors, the

Table 5-7. Sloan MBAs: Reported Stress in the Workplace.

	Female n = 65	Male n = 121
Sources of Stress (Stressors)[a]	n = 56	n = 87
Work overload	29%	16%
Inadequacy in job	37%	13%
Role ambiguity	36%	18%
Nonrecognition	12%	3%
Nonsupportive supervisor	7%	7%
Loss of discretionary responsibility	9%	6%
Work organization issues	14%	16%
Coping Strategies[a]		
Change jobs	16%	9%
Vacation	5%	5%
Discuss with supervisor	16%	3%
Discuss with family/spouse	16%	6%
Discuss with friends	11%	1%
Ignore (detachment)	9%	15%
Sought medical assistance	9%	3%
Sought psychiatric counseling	7%	—
Physical exercise (tennis, skiing, etc.)	14%	16%
Drugs and alcohol	—	5%
Workaholic	—	6%
No Stress	14%	28%

a. Frequency of mention rather than number of individuals. Some persons have noted several categories.

proportion of women identifying sources of stress was almost double the proportion for males. Table 5-7 shows stressors and coping strategies. The coping strategies utilized by men and women were quite different. Women pursued more active strategies—discussing the problems with their supervisors, family and spouses, and friends (networking with other professional women), and changing their jobs. Men reported that they coped by ignoring the stress. Both men and women participated in physical exercise (tennis, jogging, biking, skiing, etc.) to fight stress. Women sought medical assistance or psychiatric counseling, while the men identified two coping techniques not mentioned at all by women. These were to intensify their work efforts and become workaholics, and to use alcohol and drugs. One male commented that his divorce was caused by "working 90 hours a week for two years, because it was expected and necessary to meet job task targets."

Although the questionnaire did not request specific information on health or medical status, the Sloan respondents frequently mentioned that they had reacted to stress with ulcers, muscle spasms, migraines, temporary visual impairment, excessive fatigue, hypertension, and "burn out." What do these findings presage? It is apparent that although women have reported more stress than their male counterparts, they have developed more constructive ways to deal with stress. Men appear to acknowledge less stress and have resorted to less constructive ways to cope. Many males who indicated that they ignored stress also noted that their productivity had been negatively affected in the short run or that they had decided that work would not be a priority for them. Thus, the story of the Sloan MBAs may be that although women report more stress, their coping strategies appear to be more effective than those of males, and the long-term implications of stress are yet to be determined.

MENTORING

One interpersonal relationship in the workplace that appears to present more difficulties for female than for male managers is mentoring. Hunt and Michael note that "mentorship in the work environment is a complex issue involving organizational, occupational, positional, and interpersonal variables that set the scene for stages that occur during the mentor-protégé relationships."[12] Kram divides the mentoring function into two broad categories, career functions and psychosocial functions. Such functions as sponsorship, exposure, visibility, coaching, protection, and challenging assignments enhance career achievements. Psychosocial functions such as role modeling, acceptance, confirmation, counseling, and friendship enhance a sense of competence, identity, and effectiveness in a professional role.[13] Nevertheless, the scholarly literature on mentoring is riddled with a lack of conceptual clarity.

Roche noted in his study of top executives that nearly two-thirds had mentors and these executives earned more money at a younger age and were happier with their career progress.[14] Women managers also believe that mentors are helpful to their careers, but that they must contend with some issues that are unique to being a female in a predominately male organizational context. Since mentors are usually older, more experienced individuals, the scarcity of senior women limits opportunities for female mentor/female protégé relationships. The perceived problems associated with cross-gender mentoring may also be substantial enough to handicap the career success of young women managers. The Sloan women MBAs, many of whom are still fairly young, articulated a fear that a career-oriented mentoring relationship with a male might be perceived as a more intimate personal relationship. Their preference was not to be aggressive in seeking a male mentor.

The fifth year survey of Sloan School graduates included a number of questions on mentoring. The time span of five years is likely to capture most mentor relationships in their cultivation phase—"a period of two to five years when the range of career functions and psychosocial functions expand to a maximum."[15] A larger proportion of female MBAs than males reported that they had a mentor. About two-thirds of the women who responded to the mentoring questions had mentors compared to 45 percent of the men (forty-one women out of sixty-four and 53 males our of 118). The chi square equals 8.41, which is significant at the 1.5 percent level. The overwhelming number of respondents reported positive mentor/protégé relationships which had been established in a variety of ways. (For more detail see Appendix A, questions 39–53.) About three-fourths of the Sloan MBAs reported that they had had a mentor in the past, usually from a previous job or employer. Although contacts with these individuals were infrequent, they were important to Sloans when making strategic decisions on their careers.

Mentors are mostly males who hold supervisory and senior management positions in firms and are about twelve years older than their protégés. Current mentors for the Sloans have been associated with their protégés about two and one-half years and are perceived as performing a useful function. But asked what it is that mentors do, men and women have quite different responses. Both men and women reported mentors as coaches and advisors, but men provided detailed responses such as (1) "guidance in a political labyrinth both inside and outside the organization," (2) "exposure to key management," (3) "career input," (4) "feedback on work," (5) "philosophical and pragmatic brainstorming," (6) "advising best approach," (7) "protecting me from infighting." The responses of the women lack this specificity; they said a mentor (1) "gives advice," (2) "helps me to be more realistic about goals," (3) "very supportive," (4) "specific advice," (5) "has given me the projects which require technical expertise." Most of the women from the classes of 1975–77, the first two years of the survey, who responded to the mentoring questions did not have a mentor. Thus, as late as 1980–82, when these women were sending in their five-year follow-up surveys, young women managers were not in mentoring relationships. Most of the affirmative responses to mentoring for women were concentrated in the classes of 1978 and 1979. This skewed distribution might reflect the lag in the acceptance of the strictly professional male mentor/female protégé relationship.

In the regression results of MBA fifth year compensation, mentoring was identified as a significant variable. However, when separate regressions were done for male MBAs and female MBAs, mentoring remained significant for male, but not for female MBAs. Are the complexities of cross-gender mentor-protégé relationships so overwhelming that young women managers find them too difficult? Kram notes in her study that "both men and women allude to the sexual tensions and fears of increasing intimacy that cause anxiety, ambivalence, and confusion in their relationships with colleagues of the other sex."[16] Public scrutiny increases the level of stress in a mentor-protégé relationship, due to undue accusation of sexual involvement and favoritism versus competence.

Since the male/female mentoring relationship may be risky, many have asked whether a female/female relationship would enhance the career development of more junior women. In her study of mentoring between executive women and junior women managers, Fischl found that although senior women acknowledged mentoring as critical to their success, they were reluctant to provide similar support to younger women.[17] The senior women had achieved their status through hard work, long hours, and good mentoring by males. Their reluctance to mentor junior women seemed to stem from fears of being displaced by the younger, highly educated women as well as some anxiety about actual and perceived risks associated with being highly visible and not secure enough in their own positions. They expressed resentment that they were expected to help junior women because they were women: "I have been very careful to give men the same opportunities as women." From another: "The young women are a strange phenomenon. They are taught to believe that they can do any job, not limited by their sex, but they go beyond that, they want to get there faster and expect the organization to cooperate with their career plan which may not be in the context of the organization's goals and objections." While the junior women expressed a desire to be mentored by senior women, they were aware of the difficulties.

> My experience, and I have worked for three women, is that women themselves are not in senior enough positions, and/or they have not been senior very long, and/or they subconsciously feel they did not have much help along the way, so they themselves make poor mentors. They (1) may not wish to share the glory, (2) tend to need to restate their uniqueness, (3) are not secure enough in themselves and their position to be able to give help to younger, eager, aggressive junior people.

The junior women are trying to improve the situation by mentoring women who are behind them, and they have suggested that professional women's organizations would seem to provide a less threatening meeting place for junior and senior women to interact.

Another perspective on mentoring as a significant variable in career success is based on the author's survey and discussion with senior women managers (in engineering, manufacturing, marketing) in a large high technology firm with scattered facilities. Most of the women indicated that mobility within the company had been easy for them and that they had managed without a mentor. Several reported having had a short-term mentor. While mentoring in the standard sense did not necessarily play a major role in assisting these women, it was evident that networking did. One woman noted, "I participate in and lead many networks and spend much time sharing information across a wide, cross-organizational system of colleagues, subordinates, friends, supervisors, and bosses—it is critical to survival and success." These women represent a group of older managers (forty-one years is the average age), who are committed to the work ethic (forty-eight hours per week). They are successful and have risen to top levels in the company, enjoyed challenges, and have learned to "work the system." They have established networks and have identified "short-term mentors," who have enabled them to participate in the highly mobile company culture. They were aware of the need to solicit information and were not hampered by set channels for interactions.

When comparing the careers of the Sloan MBAs who did not have mentors, both men and women have been as successful if not more so than those with mentors. A hierarchical relationship is an implicit assumption of the developmental literature on managers, but Sloan MBAs have worked for management consulting firms, for investment banks, and in high technology, where there is a minimum of hierarchy. The emphasis is on the entrepreneurial mode, and work is performed on a project basis. In such unstructured work settings, learning from peers or members of the team has been crucial. Also, exposure to and interaction with principals, managing partners, or more senior personnel has been transitory. Thus, the role of mentoring in such organizations would differ from larger, more bureaucratic environments in which both mentor and protégé anticipate a more stable and longer term association.

Both women and minorities have developed surrogate mentoring relationships. Women have extensively utilized networking. These networks may be across functional lines in a company, but available only to persons at a given level, as the senior women's group (actually called the Senior Women's Group) discussed above. Professional networks which are external to a company may be functional—that is, women engineers, or cut across functional and industry lines—executive women. Also, in many dual career marriages, it is apparent that partners who are managers or professionals act as surrogate mentors to their spouses. The Sloan female MBAs see these networks as safe havens in which they might exchange information and receive advice and support from women managers who are much like themselves. Some, however, reject networking as an indication of personal shortcomings.

As long as senior executives report that mentors were crucial to their upward mobility, junior managers will strive to replicate their success. Based on the Sloan School data, lacking a mentor will not necessarily restrict achievement. But if mentoring is essential, it is apparent that both women and minorities will have a more difficult time getting the requisite treatment. There is also a need to know about mentor/protégé relationships in the less hierarchial environments in which many MBAs work.

PROFILES OF SLOAN DUAL CAREER COUPLES

Dual career couples are those individuals who pursue separate careers and at the same time share a family life together. Ninety-seven persons (forty-five women and fifty-two men) of the 203 employed respondents in the five-year survey identified themselves as dual career partners. Since 125 of the 203 individuals reported that they were married, this means that approximately 78 percent of married respondents could be classified as dual career couples. These numbers are not exact, however, since a few of the respondents noted that they were in dual career relationships and were not married. The Halls have defined dual career couples as families in which each partner has a separate work role and the lifestyle of the couple is designed to support, encourage, and facilitate—not just tolerate—the career pursuits of both members. For the analysis that follows, dual career couples do not have to be married.[18]

Although 57 percent of the men reported that they were dual "career" partners, some were in fact dual "earner" partners, with spouses employed in traditional female occupations such as librarian, nurse, public school teacher, and programmer. Career has been characterized by Cherpas as a large investment of time and energy in job training, high personal salience, substantial ego involvement, and a continuous developmental quantity where advances in responsibility, power, pay, and status accrue over time.[19] Whatever occupations these wives pursued, their partners overwhelmingly (61 percent) reported that their spouses' careers had not progressed as far as theirs. A much higher proportion of married women (over 90 percent) were in dual career relationships, and only twenty-eight percent indicated that their partners had progressed further in their careers. (See Table 5–8.)

In addition, six of the women at the time of the five-year survey were part-time workers, while all of the males in dual career relationships were full-time employees. Inclusion of the women part-timers in the dual career group reduces both the fifth year salaries and the hours of work for the group. The presence of some part-time women workers in dual career relationships would seem to support the hypothesis that women subordinate their career goals to their roles as parent and spouse. In our study the conflict between work and family roles is resolved by less than full-time participation at work for some women, or as several indicated, putting their careers temporarily on "hold."

Sixteen of the ninety-seven Sloan dual career members had met as classmates at the Sloan School and three others had attended the Sloan School at the same time that their prospective partners were at the Harvard Business School. This Sloan School subgroup of career couples did not differ from other dual career couples in this study. Almost half of the dual career respondents in the fifth year survey classified themselves as single when they graduated from the Sloan School. Over 90 percent of the other half who were married at the time of graduation did not have children. Both the single and married graduates had background characteristics that were similar to those of their non-dual career classmates at graduation.

When the research on Sloan School graduates was started in 1975, persons in dual career relationships were just beginning to emerge as a recognizable group in the managerial professions. The Rapoports had described the dual career family in 1969, but it was not until the mid- to late 1970s, with the significant increase in the number of women MBAs, that private employers became aware of the trend.[20] The initial and two-year surveys focused on job achievement and career success, but at an early stage, both men and women respondents had identified dual career issues as significant in their work and non-work activities. At the end of their second year of employment, the dual career couples had more difficulty integrating their work and non-work activities than did their classmates, and women partners in these relationships experienced more problems than male partners. At this point, women more frequently described their dual career relationships in negative terms, as providing conflict with the excessive demands of jobs that required considerable travel and long hours. Thus, at year two, most of these relationships were adversarial in the sense used by the Halls, "both partners are highly involved in their careers and only minimally involved in home, family, or partner support roles.[21]

Some of these dual career associations did not survive. The Nadelsons, a dual career couple in psychiatry, have cited clinical examples noting the dynamics of guilt, anxiety, depression, and self-esteem in dual career couples with respect to work.[22] The Johnsons, an anthropologist and a psychiatrist and another dual career couple, have noted that dual career partners may be faced with continual conflict over power, so that competition becomes quite pronounced: "In

Table 5-8. Dual Career Couples–Five-Year Survey.[a]

Variable	Male	Female
Total Number	52	45[b]
1. Hours/week	51.6	48
2. Current salary (5th year)	$48,653	$43,457
3. Stress (Scale 1 → 5)	2.56	2.78
4. Time spent with children during work week	2.45 hrs.	4.07 hrs.
	Percent	*Percent*
5. Marital Status at Fifth Year	*100*	*100*
Married	92	98
Not married	8	2
6. Have children at Fifth Year	27	42
7. Care of children[c]	*100*	*100*
Spouse	8	—
Sitter	15	63
Day care	23	25
School	39	—
Other	15	12
8. Household duties	*100*	*100*
Shared	65	46
Spouse	20	4
Self	11	30
Other	4	20
9. Spouse progress in career compared to you	*100*	*100*
a. Progressed further	12	35
b. As far	27	49
c. Not as far	61	16
10. Your career affects relationship	*100*	*100*
Problems	39	23
No problems	31	16
Helps	30	61
11. Spouse career affect relationship	*100*	*100*
Problems	31	32
No problems	36	34
Helps	33	34

Table 5-8. continued

Variable	Male	Female
	Percent	*Percent*
12. Your relationship affect job	*100*	*100*
Constrains	25	42
No effect	42	16
Helps	29	40
Both helps and constrains	4	2
13. Career aspirations	*100*	*100*
Lowered	19	42
Increased	6	23
Other[d]	75	35
14. Job and personal life interfere	*100*	*100*
A lot	35	28
Some	33	30
Not much	27	33
Other	5	9

a. See fifth year survey—Appendix B.
b. Includes six part-time employees.
c. Information on ages of children available but not coded.
d. Aspirations more sharply focused.

themselves, high commitment careers are learned and conducted in a highly competitive atmosphere. Both participants must maintain a level of productivity which can equal or outdistance their colleagues. To have both marital partners engage in these careers often extends this competitiveness into the intimately and reciprocal interaction in the marriage."[23] The Halls noted that it was not uncommon to find achievement-oriented people married to each other. They may sense greater urgency in accomplishing job tasks, invest more of themselves in their careers, and take on more pressures. If both partners are bringing home job stresses, the entire relationship may consist simply of coping with work pressures. This is typical of young couples just launching their careers.[24]

By the time of the fifth year survey, most of the Sloan dual career couples had become allies with considerable reduction of conflict in career and domestic activities. Over three-fourths of the Sloan dual career couples reported that their partners were the most supportive person in their lives, a much higher proportion than their classmates. Also, only about one-third indicated that there was a lot of interference between their jobs and their personal activities. Other questions on the fifth year survey which were designed to focus on dual career couples inquired about child care arrangements, sharing of household chores, and the career progression of each partner. Four questions concerned career progression: (1) How has your dual career affected your progress or performance at work (that is, does it constrain, have no effect, facilitate, etc.)? (2) Has your spouse progressed as far in his/her career as you have? (3) How has your career affected your dual career relationship? and (4) How has your spouse's career affected the relationship?

The Sloan men and women dual career couples are compared with each other as well as with their married and not married classmates. A higher percentage of dual career women than dual career males have children. This reflects the inclusion of part-time women, most of whom have adjusted their work schedules to take care of small children. A smaller percentage of dual career males have children than their traditional married male counterparts (29 versus 100 percent). The traditional males relied heavily on spouses at home to take care of children, while children of dual career males depend on schools and day care centers with very few spouses assuming main responsibility for child care. Women dual career members indicated that they relied on sitters and day care centers. (See Table 5–8.)

Sixty-five percent of the dual career males reported that they shared household responsibilities, more than double the percentage of traditional males. Half of the dual career women either do household chores themselves (30 percent) or have others, usually paid workers (20 percent) do the work. However, sharing of household responsibilities does not necessarily entail a fifty-fifty arrangement. The typical sharing arrangement for a Sloan School dual career couple was 70 percent female and 30 percent for male. Although responses were not coded by type of chore, males reported activities such as cutting the grass, taking out the garbage, and painting the house, while women assumed most of the cooking, cleaning, and household managerial responsibilities.

The major accommodation with respect to household responsibilities was left to women. The Johnsons stated that "It must be remembered also that husbands in dual career marriages usually espouse norms on women's equality and are usually rather supportive in terms of concrete assistance. However, since they usually place a higher priority on their own careers and since they are likely to make more money, their careers are rarely sacrificed for the family or for their wives' careers."[25] Since the Sloan dual career couples were just learning how to perform in their roles in the mid- to late 1970s, it is likely that a decade later, there is either a better division of labor or more reliance on paid assistance, and/or utilization of more time-saving devices such as microwave ovens or fully prepared meals from specialized vendors.

What has been the effect, given the stresses and the additional effort required to manage a dual career relationship, on the individual careers of the partners? Only partial answers can be derived from these data. Sixty percent of the male dual career respondents reported that their partners had not made as much progress as they had in their careers. Thirty-five percent of the dual career women indicated that their partners were further along, and another 49 percent reported as much progress in their careers as their husbands. (See Figure 5-2.) With few exceptions, these are young couples who have recently launched their careers. Perhaps it is already determined that these dual career relationships, if maintained, will continue to develop along these career paths with men remaining the major achievers.

Dual career partners had significantly different answers to the question of how the dual career relationship had affected their performance at work, with 42 percent of the women reporting that it constrained their work performance and 42 percent of the men reporting that a dual career relationship had no effect on their job. When asked how their careers had affected the dual career relationship, women (60 percent) overwhelmingly reported that it had helped, as compared with only 30 percent of the men who perceived their careers as helpful to the relationship. A higher percentage of men (39 percent) saw their careers as creating problems for the relationship as compared with only 23 percent of the women. These differences might reflect that women are more inclined to be accommodative in order to manage a dual career relationship. A significantly higher proportion of dual career women had lowered their career aspirations as compared with men, 42 percent against 19 percent; this is shown in Table 5-8.

Figure 5-2. Sloan Dual Career Couple Comparisons.

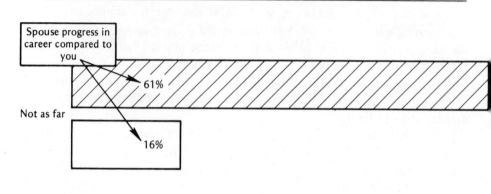

Spouse progress in career compared to you

61%

Not as far

16%

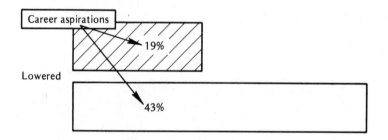

Career aspirations

19%

Lowered

43%

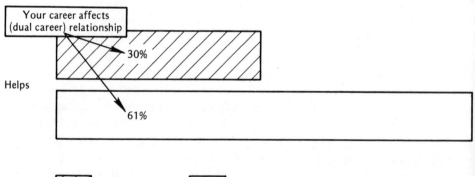

Your career affects (dual career) relationship

30%

Helps

61%

⧄ – Male   ☐ – Female

The data provides information on a dual career relationship as reported by one partner only. Each member of the eight dual career couples where each was a Sloan School graduate preferred individual interviews. There was corroboration of what the other partner had stated. Also, several males identified themselves as dual career partners, but noted that they had specifically selected a mate who worked nine to five, with no overtime, and few travel requirements. Thus it might appear that males, regardless of their espoused ideals, feel less comfortable in dual career relationships with both members in high commitment careers. The Johnsons have written that,

> Today there is a widespread cultural mandate among members of the upper-middle class, that bright and talented women should not bury their talents in domestic and child-rearing concerns. Instead, they should compete with men by engaging in high commitment careers. At the same time, women are still expected to marry, to have children, and to retain their stereotypic femininity. In order to satisfy these incongruent cultural directives, increasing numbers of men and women are attempting to fashion a new family form, where both partners are engaged in dual roles, which demand an extraordinary expenditure of time and energy.[26]

From this study, it is clear that Sloan MBAs who are in dual career relationships have additional responsibilities directly related to these relationships.

COMPARISON OF SLOAN AND OTHER MBA SALARIES

Salaries of Sloan MBAs over a five-year period were compared with results from studies of MBAs from the University of Chicago, Columbia University, Stanford University, the University of Pittsburgh, and Pace University. Reder's salary regressions of 758 MBAs from the University of Chicago for the period 1971–74 found that the starting salary ($14,641) positively associated with previous work experience and grade point averages.[27] Starting salaries for female MBAs (7 percent of the sample) were lower mainly because of smaller rewards for prior work experience. The salary disadvantage tended to decline each year as women improved their quality—that is, grade point averages and prior work experience. In other published studies of MBAs, neither grade point average nor the scores on Graduate Management Aptitude Tests (GMATs) have been significant variables for salaries.

The industry of employment distribution for University of Chicago MBAs differed from that of the Sloan MBAs. For the Chicago MBAs, accounting represented 14 percent of employment, commercial banking 21 percent, consulting 5 percent, other financial institutions 7 percent, and 53 percent in all other, mainly manufacturing.[28] To some extent this distribution reflects the different time periods of the studies and perhaps the functional specialties of the two management schools.

In 1980, Devanna matched forty-five male and forty-five female MBA graduates from the classes of 1969–72 at Columbia University and examined their career patterns and salaries over the decade following graduation.[29] Men and women MBAs, matched by age, year of graduation, work experience, and areas of concentration received the same salary in their entry level positions and were distributed in comparable proportions by industrial sector and functional areas. She found that,

> after ten years, there was still no significant difference in the number of men and women to be found in any given average sector or functional area. There was, however, a significant difference in average salaries paid in different industry sectors. In addition, there was a significant difference between what men earn and what women earn in the highest paying industry sector, manufacturing. While there was no significant difference in pay in the different functional areas, there was an interaction effect between income, functional area, and sex. This meant men earn significantly more than women when they work in the financial function.[30]

Salaries at entry level of $14,355 for men and $14,068 for women were nearly the same. Salaries for the tenth year of post-school work experience (but collected in 1980, rather than ten years after the classes work 1969–72 had graduated) show that men have averaged $49,356 and women $40,022 annually. While the salaries of women in finance had kept pace with men, their salaries had fallen furthest behind men in manufacturing, the highest paying sector. Devanna concluded that the wage gap that emerged over time could not be attributed to different motivational patterns around their work careers. An interesting comment was that the spouse earnings may provide a motivational deterrent to achievement for women. The study concluded that the major impediment to equal pay for men and women of equal credentials and background lies not in their levels of motivation but rather in societal and organizational phenomena.[31]

Several studies of MBAs from Stanford University also showed salary differences between men and women. Gordon and Strober surveyed 131 MBAs (including eighteen women) from the 1974 class of Stanford Graduate School of Business and found that although the starting salaries of men at $17,000 and of women at $16,938 were equal, the women's long-term salary and wealth aspirations were below those of the men.[32] The 176 MBA graduates of the Class of 1974 responded to another survey four years later and reported that males earned a mean annual salary of $27,787 and females $25,657, not a significant difference at the 5 percent level. However, when additional bonuses and other cash compensation were added to the salary, the difference between male compensation of $34,762 and female compensation of $27,455 was significant. The most important determinant of salary was industry of employment. No women were employed in the two highest paying industries, investment banking and real estate. In addition, the higher percentage of women who had been out of the labor force one month or more during the four-year period had a significant negative effect on salary, almost a $9,000 reduction in income in 1978 when other variables in the regression were held constant.[33] These studies tend to support a thesis of occupational rather than wage discrimination.

Several detailed studies of income differentials between male and female MBAs at the University of Pittsburgh provide a contrast to the graduates of Sloan and other management schools listed among the top ten. The University of Pittsburgh is a large urban university with many part-time students attending its business school. Olson and Frieze have focused on job area and industry as possible determinants of both starting and subsequent MBA salaries. Their study examines whether starting salary has a significant impact on later salaries and whether prior work experience has any additional impact on current salary once one controls for starting salary. The research was based on responses from 1,433 MBAs who had graduated from the University of Pittsburgh during the period from 1973 to 1982. The respondents provided information on job title and industry of employment prior to entering the MBA program, starting job after graduation, and present (early 1984) job. Unlike the Sloan pool of MBAs, Pittsburgh included graduates from the executive MBA programs (101 individuals), foreign students, and part-time workers (504 individuals). Their average age of thirty-four years at the time of the report placed them in an older cohort than Sloan MBAs, who after five years of post-MBA work experience averaged under thirty-two years of age.[34]

The 984 males in the Pittsburgh sample started at $2,000 more in salary than their 449 female counterparts, and by 1983, the males earned about $9,200 more. Gross salary including bonus was $44,500 for men and $35,300 for women. When job area, job level, industry, and prior work experience variables were included in the MBA earnings function, the salary gap between men and women in 1983 was reduced to $2,170. Olson and Frieze added starting salaries to the regression equation, and found that the coefficients for sex, while continuing to be negative, were statistically insignificant; thus, a lower starting salary seemed to be the major explanation for the 1983 salary differential. About 50 percent of the gender differential in starting salaries was explained by job area, job level, industry, and type of prior work experience.[35] If starting salary is a proxy for occupational discrimination, it is not surprising that the sex discrimination becomes important.

Salary comparisons of MBAs from other business schools have not been investigated as extensively. Harlan and Jelinek's report on the success of Harvard MBAs from the classes of 1960–75 noted that women lagged their male colleagues in starting salary and that the gap increased over time. Male graduates of the 1960s earned a median income of $3,000 to $4,000 per month compared to $2,000 to $3,000 for women. For the graduates of the 1970s, women lagged behind men by $1,500 to $2,000 per month. This study did not have compensation as a primary focus, and it was conducted before women became a significant percentage of the Harvard MBAs.[36]

However, women MBAs from the Harvard Business School have been well covered in *Fortune* and *Business Week*. In August 1978, *Fortune* reviewed the progress of the thirty-four women (4.4 percent of the class) who were graduated in 1973, and again at their tenth anniversary in 1983. *Fortune* reported that thirty-three of the women MBAs from the class of 1973 were working and with one exception, all worked full time. Their median income in 1983 was $57,000, but they lagged behind their male peers from Harvard, 35 percent of whom earned over $100,000.[37] Had data been available to test determinants of Harvard MBA salaries, it is likely that this wage gap would have been smaller.

Pace University is an urban university with many part-time students. Reitman's research on the progress of MBAs reported equal pay for men and women. Two hundred and seven MBAs from the classes of 1976–80 who were employed on a full-time basis in 1984 comprised the study group. Average salaries for men was $54,000 and $49,100 for women. The explanatory variables in annual salary were: the year the MBA was received, full-time experience prior to the MBA, hours worked per week, number of career interruptions, and primary job responsibility in finance. Reitman concluded that four to eight years after receipt of the MBA, men and women were doing equally well with their careers and had equal salaries.[38]

Sloan School MBAs have fared well during the first five years of post-management school experience. The 56 percent salary increase for both men and women may indicate that these MBAs represent the larger universe of managers with MBAs, who now include about a third of all managers. Female MBAs had starting salaries equal to those of their male peers and after five years of work experience still had comparable pay. However, women paid a higher price for their success in that they experienced more job-related stress, and that some had become part-time workers. Although industry of employment remained a significant variable, by the fifth year women were moving away from manufacturing and other good-paying industries to the lower paid, other services category. The Sloan School MBAs enjoyed considerable economic achievement, and remained generally satisfied with their status.

NOTES

1. U.S. Bureau of the Census, *Money, Income and Poverty Status of Families and Persons in the United States, 1984*, Series P. 60, No. 149 (Washington, D.C.: U.S. Government Printing Office, 1985).

2. Beginning salaries based on data from the Placement Office of the Sloan School of Management at MIT.

3. Arthur M. Okun, *Prices and Quantities* (Washington, D.C.: The Brookings Institution, 1981).

4. Placement Office of the Sloan School of Management at MIT.

5. Abraham Maslow, "A Theory of Human Motivation," *Psychological Review* 50 (1943): 370–96; Chris Argyris, *Personality and Organization* (New York: Harper, 1957); Frederick Herzberg, *Work and the Nature of Man* (New York: World, 1966); David McClelland, "Toward A Theory of Motive Acquisition," *American Psychologist* 20 (1965): 321–33; Douglas McGregor, *The Human Side of Enterprise* (New York: McGraw-Hill, 1960); Daniel Yankelovich, *The New Rules* (New York: Random House, 1981); Terence Mitchell, "Expectancy Models of Job Satisfaction, Occupational Preference and Effort: A Theoretical, Methodological and Empirical Appraisal," *Psychological Bulletin* 81 (1974) 1053–1077; Rosabeth M. Kantor, *Men and Women of the Corporation* (New York: Basic Books, 1977).

6. Jeffrey Pfeffer, "Effects of an MBA and Socio-economic Origins in Business Schools Graduates' Salaries," *Journal of Applied Psychology* 62 (1977): 698–703.

7. "The Street Is Still Mecca for B-School Grads," *Business Week*, December 22, 1986.

8. "Employers Offer Aid On Child Care," *The New York Times*, January 17, 1988.

9. John Ivancevich and Michael Matteson, *Stress and Work: A Managerial Perspective* (Glenview, Ill.: Scott, Foresman and Co., 1980), p. 103.

10. Cathleen R. Tilney, *Stress and MBA's*, Master's thesis, Sloan School of Management at MIT, June 1982.

11. Anne Harlan and Carol Weiss, "Sex Differences in Factors Affecting Managerial Career Advancement," in P.A. Wallace, ed., *Women in the Workplace* (Boston: Auburn House Publishing Co., 1982), pp. 88–94.

12. David Marshall Hunt and Carol Michael, "Mentorship: A Career Training and Development Tool," *Academy of Management Review* 8 (1983): 475–85.

13. Kathy E. Kram, *Mentoring at Work: Developmental Relationships and Organizational Life* (Glenview, Ill.: Scott, Foresman and Co., 1985), pp. 22–46.

14. Gerard E. Roche, "Much Ado About Mentors," *Harvard Business Review* 57 (1979): 17–28.

15. Kram, *Mentoring at Work*, p. 53.

16. Ibid., p. 105.

17. Patricia W. Fischl, "Mentoring and Developmental Relationships Between Senior Executive Women and Junior Female Managers," Master's thesis, Sloan School of Management at MIT, 1986.

18. Francine S. Hall and Douglas T. Hall, *The Two-Career Couple* (Reading, Mass.: Addison-Wesley Publishing Company, 1979, p. 10.

19. Catherine C. Cherpas, "Dual Career Families: Terminology, Typologies, and Work and Family Issues," *Journal of Counseling and Development* 83 (June 1985): 616.

20. Rhona Rapoport and Robert N. Rapoport, "The Dual Career Family," *Human Relations* 11 (1969): 3-30; Rhona Rapoport and Robert N. Rapoport, *Dual Career Families* (Harmondsworth, England: Penguin Books, 1971).

21. Hall and Hall, *Two-Career Couple*, p. 24.

22. Carol C. Nadelson and Theodore Nadelson, "Dual-Career Marriages: Benefits and Costs," in F. Pepitone-Rockwell, ed., *Dual-Career Couples* (Beverly Hills: Sage Publications, 1980), pp. 91-109.

23. Colleen Leahy Johnson and Frank A. Johnson, "Parenthood, Marriage, and Careers: Situational Constraints and Role Strain," in F. Pepitone-Rockwell ed., *Dual-Career Couples* (Beverly Hills: Sage Publications, 1980) p. 149.

24. Hall and Hall, *Two-Career Couple*, p. 98.

25. Johnson and Johnson, "Parenthood," p. 158.

26. Ibid., p. 143.

27. M.W. Reder, "An Analysis of a Small Closely Observed Labor Market: Starting Salaries for University of Chicago MBAs," *Journal of Business* 51 (1978): 263-97.

28. Ibid., p. 268.

29. Mary Anne Devanna, *Male/Female Careers: The First Decade, A Study of MBAs* (New York: Center for Research in Career Development, Columbia University, Graduate School of Business, 1984).

30. Ibid., p. 4.

31. Ibid., p. 5.

32. Francine E. Gordon and Myra H. Strober, "Initial Observations On a Pioneer Cohort: 1974 Women MBAs," *Sloan Management Review* 19 (Winter 1978): 15-23.

33. Myra H. Strober, "The MBA: Same Passport to Success for Women and Men?" in P. Wallace, ed., *Women in the Workplace* (Boston: Auburn House Publishing Company, 1982), pp. 25-44.

34. Josephine E. Olson, Irene H. Frieze, and Deborah C. Good," The Effects of Job Type and Industry on the Income of Male and Female MBAs," *The Journal of Human Resources* 22 (Fall 1987): 532-41.

35. Ibid.

36. Anne Harlan and Mariann Jelinek, "Women in Management: A Study of Graduates of the Harvard Business School," (Paper presented at meeting of the Academy of Management, Kansas City, Missouri, 1976).

37. "How Harvard's Women MBAs Are Managing," *Fortune*, 11 July 1983.

38. Frieda Reitman, "MBA Career Paths—Are They Different for Men and Women? A Study of Pace University's Graduates," (Paper presented at Academy of Management, San Diego, Calif., August 1985).

6 MINORITY MANAGERS
A Slower Path to Recognition

The analysis in this chapter is based on the experiences of blacks who completed the two-year program and received a Master of Science in management degree from the Sloan School at MIT. Some of the statistical series may also include a small number of minorities other than blacks. Although the success, or lack thereof, of black managers in the private sector has been assessed during the past twenty years, there is hardly any consensus on how many black managers are in this area.

A literature search revealed several limited surveys, some personal histories and anecdotes from black managers, studies of black managers in special industries such as banks and telecommunications, and a plethora of articles on how to survive in the corporate jungle. Official statistics from the Bureau of Labor Statistics and the Equal Employment Opportunity Commission (EEOC) cover different categories of managers. In 1965, blacks and other minorities accounted for almost 3 percent of the 7 million executive, administrative, and managerial employees in the United States.[1] This broad category included managers in all levels of government (public sector) and self-employed individuals, as well as managers in the private sector. Fifteen years later, these minority managers made up approximately 5 percent of the managerial and executive work force. However, black managers only were 3.7 percent of all managers in 1980.[2]

Since 1966, the Equal Employment Opportunity Commission has collected employment data, by race and sex, from large private corporations. The coverage of these data are limited in that only employers with 100 or more employees and certain federal contractors with 50 or more employees are required to file annual reports (EEO-1). In 1985, the EEOC reported 133,029 black male and 82,114 black female officials and managers. They represented 4.8 percent of all officials and managers.[3] The officials and managers category is a broad classification, including numerous levels of responsibility from the manager of the photocopy room to the chief executive officer of a Fortune 500 company. Nevertheless, black managers have remained a small percent of all managers throughout the period of strong implementation of anti-discrimination laws in employment.

Black MBAs have been an increasing proportion of all black managers. The Council for Opportunity in Graduate Management Education (COGME) was started in 1970 to expedite the entry of blacks into managerial positions by providing fellowships for blacks to pursue graduate degrees. Between 1970 and 1980, approximately 2,000 black MBAs were graduated from the ten participating COGME schools.[4] A smaller consortium of six universities[5] may have graduated a third as many black MBAs during this decade.

The National Center for Educational Statistics reported that 1,549 MBAs were conferred on blacks (1,231 to men and 318 to women) attending institutions of higher education in the United States in 1975–76. They accounted for 4.1 percent of all MBAs granted that year. By 1980–82, the 2,359 black MBAs (1,554 men and 805 women) remained 4.1 percent of all MBAs. The twenty-four minority graduates (classes of 1975–79) who have provided the data for the Sloan School's five-year longitudinal analysis are representative of that small but elite category of black managers who have received degrees from the leading management schools. Compared to their peers from the Sloan School, how did they fare after five years? The overwhelming consensus of all studies of black managers is that blacks have not done as well in the corporate world as their white counterparts. After a review of the literature, the study attempted to determine why, after five years, minority Sloan MBAs received significantly lower salaries than their white counterparts. What were the reasons for the "invisible ceilings" on their upward mobility?

LITERATURE REVIEW

The literature on blacks in management is sparse and emphasizes attitudes rather than experiences. Nevertheless, a review of that literature of the past two decades provides a general context for a study of minority Sloan MBAs. One of the first attempts to evaluate the career paths of black professionals in the private sector was undertaken in 1971 in research supported by the U.S. Department of Labor.[6] The 500 black male professionals in the survey were well educated, with 12 percent holding MBA degrees. They were mostly under thirty-five years of age and were employed in a wide variety of industries in the private sector, with 42 percent in manufacturing. Because the study was designed to investigate the progress of black male college graduates in private industry, the more encompassing occupational group of "professional, technical, and managerial," revealed relatively few in managerial positions. Three out of five surveyed felt that there was a ceiling on how far they could go in their firms, and the ceiling was rather low. Comments from some of their white supervisors tended to reinforce the pessimism of these black professionals concerning future opportunities in their firms.[7]

Another researcher, Fernandez, conducted research in 1971–72 on black managers in corporations with mostly white employees.[8] A sample of 116 black managers and a comparison group of 156 white managers in eight firms in California (two banks, two public utilities, and four manufacturing companies) were surveyed to assess the careers of black managers. Fernandez found that most of the black managers were in lower management positions and performing jobs generally associated with black consumer markets and/or black employees. Salaries of black managers lagged behind those of white managers, and a large percentage of black managers indicated that racial discrimination was the primary factor affecting their careers. White managers, in these firms, saw the major explanations for the scarcity of black managers as cultural differences and the lack of necessary qualifications.[9]

Although many companies, under some external pressures, have hired black managers, these employees remain in the lower ranks and their promotions lag considerably behind those for their white male peers. The black managers in the Fernandez study indicated that hostile internal environments and the negative attitudes of peers, subordinates, and supervisors were significant factors affecting their career progress. Both black and white managers in the study believed that "college education, technical knowledge, and an MBA were essential in both principle and practice for promotions."[10] However, many of the managers believed that non-ability related factors such as age, sex, race, and national origin also play crucial roles in the promotional opportunities of managers. Fifty-three percent of the white managers believed that blacks must be better than whites to get ahead, and/or that the firms were more careful in promoting blacks because they wanted to be certain that blacks would succeed.[11]

Brown and Ford examined the progress of black MBAs. They surveyed 161 of the 227 minority MBAs, mostly black, who had graduated from the "consortium" universities between 1969 and 1974, and twenty black MBAs from two predominately black colleges. The study concluded that although the MBA made a difference in the rate at which minority members entered corporate business, these managers, even after four to five years were still in the lowest levels of the corporation. They had not progressed as far as white MBAs.[12]

The 1978 report by America and Anderson was based on interviews with 100 black middle managers in large corporations, and addressed itself mainly as to how to be effective in corporate structures and enhance career development.[13] Shortly after these strategies for survival were delineated by America and Anderson, Heidrick and Struggles, an executive search firm, surveyed black executives.[14] In July 1979, the firm mailed questionnaires to 638 men and women identified as black executives, and 375 responded. Ninety percent were men who worked mainly in manufacturing and finance, real estate and insurance, and were well distributed across functional areas in the industries. Eighty-five percent of these black executives were college graduates and 39 percent had graduate degrees. At an average age of forty-three years, they had worked for three employers. Although they expressed an above average degree of satisfaction with their career progress, 45 percent specified racial discrimination as the single most impeding factor to their career success. Nearly six out of ten of the survey participants felt that black progress in achieving executive positions over the past fifteen years had been slower than that of women. An even greater proportion (45 percent) felt that black progress would lag that of women in the coming years.[15]

Five significant studies of black managers, published in the 1980s, have attempted to generate an understanding of intergroup relations within the context of an organization. "Diagnosing Race Relations in Management" was authored by an inter-racial team of two white researchers and two black researchers who probed the dynamics of race relations among managers in one large industrial corporation.[16] The company had 11,000 employees, of which 2,000 were managers. More than 150 of those managers were black. Although the corporation had a history of progressive actions on race relations, the director of human resources asked the assistance of an external diagnostic team to examine the relationship between black and white managers.

The diagnostic team worked with an internal advisory committee of equal race/sex composition, which represented the full range of racial attitudes within management. A questionnaire was administered to 676 managers (140 blacks and 536 whites). A fairly sophisticated analysis of the responses led the researchers to conclude "that in some key areas, black and white managers may hold cognitively different theories to explain what happens in the organizational world in which they live."[17] Generally, white managers had a more favorable view of race relations at the corporation than black managers. Blacks saw more evidence of racism. Both groups differed in their perception of the specific characteristics of the relationships between the races. Each group saw the other group as more closed than its own, and whites generally tended to perceive the impact of their behavior in relation to blacks more favorably than did blacks.[18]

On the mobility issues of hiring, evaluation, and promotion, there were substantial differences in views. Whites were less likely to believe that black managers were hired on the basis of competence and more likely to believe that they were hired soley to fill racial quotas. A substantial proportion of whites and almost all blacks believed that blacks must work harder than whites to prove themselves. Almost two-thirds of black managers believed that blacks are almost never fairly evaluated by white supervisors, while only a small proportion of white managers entertained this possibility. The greatest disagreement between black and white managers was on the perception of promotional opportunities. One finding was that in general, blacks get less career relevant information from whites than whites do, and blacks were told more often than whites that their promotional probabilities depended on their race. More than ten times the proportion of whites than blacks believed that blacks were promoted even if they were doing a mediocre job. Both groups felt that their own group was at a disadvantage on mobility and that the other group had a clear advantage.[19] Finally, blacks and whites disagreed on recommendations for the most effective way to improve race relations in the corporation, clearly indicating that the implementation and long-term success of any intervention strategy may require considerable determination by management.

The second publication by Fernandez *Racism and Sexism in Corporate Life*, in 1980, examined the atmosphere within which minority and women managers worked.[20] The shifting composition of the work force toward more heterogeneity has created new types of conflict and stress. Many minorities and women have diverse cultural backgrounds, different value systems, and different expectations than do the white males who presently dominate corporations. The "coming together" of these people of diverse backgrounds, in some cases for the first time, in the corporate setting has created great tension for everyone. Thus, a better understanding of the managers feelings, beliefs, and attitudes was the central concern of the study.

Between 1976 and 1978, Fernandez surveyed 4,202 managers who were employed in ten large companies, apparently within one corporate structure. The survey sample was stratified by race, sex, and managerial level. These companies had a combined managerial work force of over 125,000 individuals. Random selection of participants yielded 2,103 minority managers, including 907 black managers. A comprehensive overview of corporate management included specific concerns such as career planning, performance evaluation, potential evaluation, job satisfaction, work design, training, and development.

Although data were also collected from Asians, Hispanics, Native Americans, and white managers, black managers are highlighted here because they seem to be the most alienated and critical of the corporate procedures. Fernandez raises but does not answer satisfactorily, a critical question why the perceptions and views of black managers on the treatment of managers in their companies are far more critical than the views of other minority group managers. Are black managers more visible, culturally different, or have they had a longer work experience in these companies? Is the dual stigma of slavery and color so powerful that few individuals, regardless of education, achievement, and attitudes can function outside of the boundaries of the stereotypes? Fernandez asserts that the hierarchy of alienation is based in large part on whites' non-ambivalent feelings toward blacks, the size of the black population, and whites' longer experience in the labor force. Large numbers of white managers, particularly at the lower levels of management, believe that their career opportunities have been hindered since equal employment opportunity (EEO).[21] This may lead them to do things that are detrimental to blacks.

Black managers were the most critical minority group regarding the corporate treatment of minorities. More than half of black managers believed that minorities are penalized more for mistakes than are whites. Fernandez concluded: "Between 21 percent and 31 percent of the Native Americans, Asian, Hispanic, and white managers of both sexes believe that minority managers are excluded from informal work groups. By contrast, 71 percent of black men and 59 percent of black women believe this is true."[22] One of the most important findings of the study is that almost half of all managers (46 percent) believe that most white managers make minority managers feel they got their jobs because of EEO targets, rather than because of their ability.[23]

Within the corporate environment, promotions are of great concern to employees, since they provide both financial and non-financial rewards, especially the opportunity to satisfy career needs, goals, and aspirations. The study revealed the difference between the levels of expectation and aspiration of managers. Black men had the largest percentage difference between the desire to advance to upper level jobs (52 percent) and the expectation of getting there (23 percent). Finally, the study indicated that black men received the lowest overall performance ratings in their companies, and suggested that low-performing blacks are at an advantage and high-performing blacks at a disadvantage, as compared with whites.[24] The performance appraisal has been described by some as unreliable and subjective, and may be used in a discriminatory fashion. Male managers may have difficulties evaluating and giving feedback to women and similarly, white managers may have difficulties evaluating the performance of minorities. Thus, lower performing blacks may receive higher ratings than they deserve and high-performing blacks may receive lower ratings.

In 1985, Beaty and Smithers investigated the validity of career anchors for forty black technical managers and professionals from both private and public sectors.[25] Career anchors, a concept developed by Schein, states that certain self-images formed through work experience function to guide and constrain an individual's entire career. These basic self-images not only influence career choices but serve to shape what individuals are looking for in life. Schein noted at least eight types of career anchors: (1) technical/functional competence—primary motivation by content and challenge of work performed; (2) managerial competence—primary interest in managerial process of complex problems, high levels of uncertainty and conflict; (3) security-individuals, interested in careers that offer long-term organizational security and stability; (4) autonomy—individuals primarily concerned about their own sense of freedom; (5) entrepreneurial; (6) service—individual primarily concerned in working with others in a helping or supportive role; (7) pure challenge; and (8) lifestyle—people primarily concerned with integration of their own personal needs with that of family and career.[26]

Not surprisingly, Beaty and Smithers found that 45 percent of the technical black professionals and managers in their study had technical/functional career anchors. At about forty years of age, those college-educated individuals had worked for about three employers in a number of positions and had found the match between their careers and the needs of the organization. They were not significantly different from comparable whites. The real surprise was the low number of security types in this group, contrary to expectations; the authors were testing the stereotype that blacks were more risk averse and consequently, would be more security oriented.

Building on their earlier collaboration, Thomas and Alderfer have developed a conceptual framework for examining the influence of race on the career development of black managers.[27] According to their intergroup perspective, "individuals and organizations are constantly attempting . . . to manage potential conflicts arising from the interface between identity (members share common biological characteristics, historical experiences and similar world views) and organization group memberships."[28] The authors note that traditional career theorists have overlooked the importance of race on the career development of minorities, and in their work discuss some of the reasons why this field has not been included in mainstream research.[29]

The final report in this literature review on black managers is an autobiographical statement by a black manager. In an article in *Harvard Business Review* of July/August 1973, Jones discussed his experience as a black manager in a large corporation and his difficulties because of problems fitting into the informal organization.[30] A decade later, in a follow-up article assessing the progress of black managers in U.S. corporations published in the *Harvard Business Review*, Jones noted that 98 percent of the black MBA respondents to a survey believed that their corporations have not achieved equal opportunity. Some 84 percent of these respondents (107 out of 305 graduates of the top five U.S. graduate business schools) thought that considerations of race have a negative impact on ratings, pay, assignments, recognition, appraisals, and promotion.[31]

Some twenty years after the entry of significant numbers of black managers into private sector jobs, there is disenchantment and concern that ceilings have been placed on their upward mobility. Some may leave the corporate sector for entrepreneurial activities. Others may remain in the corporation but become somewhat disengaged from their work. Others will realize that labor markets reflect the social norms of the larger society and that a pioneering generation rarely benefits fully from its endeavors. As the following discussion on Sloan minority graduates will make clear, the employment context, even for the elite of minority managers, is more difficult than for white managers.

SLOAN SCHOOL MINORITY GRADUATES, 1975–79

Several definitions were used to determine the minority individuals who were included in the five-year tracking of graduates from the Sloan School. This study excluded all foreign students, who may have represented nearly a quarter of students enrolled in the two-year Master's Program. A number of non-black minorities might be in this category of foreign students, as well as a few blacks from Africa and the Caribbean. This research also excluded individuals who were enrolled in the Executive Development Programs, and designated as Sloan Fellows. Fellows may have had at least ten years of professional or managerial work experience and are sponsored by their employers. Beginning in the early 1970s, black Sloan Fellows attended this program. Thus, the definition of minority here would be mainly black students and a few non-black minorities who were recipients of COGME fellowships. These fellowships were available to blacks, Hispanics, Native Americans, and Asian Americans. Since Asian students are not underrepresented at MIT, they were not defined as minorities in this research project. Both quantitative and qualitative analyses were undertaken, and for some comparisons, eight additional black graduates from the Sloan School for the period after 1979 who responded to the surveys were included in the analysis. The sample of twenty-four black graduates and several other minorities provided detailed information on their job histories and their personal lives over a five-year period. In the statistical analyses where comparisons have been made with their white peers, only the twenty-four minorities in the classes of 1975–79 are included.

Table 6-1 shows the profile of minority Sloan MBAs in the initial survey year. Their profile is similar to that of their Sloan peers. A larger proportion of the minorities were married and had children; like their Sloan peers, they had majored in engineering, mathematics, and management in undergraduate school. Their Sloan School concentrations were heavily in finance and MIS/operations research.

The initial salary of minority MBAs was $34,322 or 95 percent of the average beginning salary of $36,149 for white Sloan MBAs (both adjusted for inflation). However, each group accepted jobs in different industries. Minority MBAs (57 percent as compared with 41 percent of the white MBAs went to Fortune 500 manufacturing and high technology companies). Minorities had little or no presence in management consulting—in fact, not a single minority male was employed in management consulting. Thus, the appropriate salary comparisons should be made only between minorities in manufacturing and high technology industries and whites in these industries. The initial salary for minorities in manufacturing and high technology was $35,762 or 99 percent of the average beginning salary of $36,157 for white MBAs. Table 6-2 shows these salary comparisons.

After two years of post-graduation work experience, the status of minority MBAs started to differ from their Sloan peers. More minorities were in staff jobs, fewer had mentors, more were dissatisfied by bureaucracy and red tape, and more felt constrained by discrimination. More minority MBAs were only moderately satisfied with their jobs and dissatisfied with their performance appraisals.*

---

*Data for the second and fifth years are not shown in separate tables as was done for women in earlier chapters. Significant differences between minority and white Sloan MBAs are reported in Table 6-3.

These were early warning signals of difficulties ahead. After two years, the income gap between the two groups in manufacturing and high technology widened. Minority MBAs received an average salary of $36,067, or 88 percent of the average salary of $41,206 received by white MBAs. This difference of $5,139 was significant (variance estimate $t = 2.85$). Nearly all of the minority MBAs reported that they had not been promoted "on time" along with their peers at work. White MBAs who may have been dissatisfied changed positions or employers, but blacks remained in their jobs.

At the end of five years, minority Sloan MBAs had not fared as well as their Sloan School counterparts. By the fifth year the average salaries of the minority MBAs had increased 29 percent, as compared with the 41 percent increase in the salaries of white MBAs. The minority MBA averages $44,380 as compared to $50,980 for white MBAs. This difference of $6,600 was significant (variance estimate $t = 2.89$) and represented 15 percent of the mean salary for minority MBAs. The top of the salary range in the fifth year was $110,000 for full-time Sloan women and $150,000 for men, but only $58,000 for male and female Sloan minorities. (These last three numbers are in current dollars; all of the other comparisons are in inflation-adjusted dollars.) The primary reason for the significant salary gap was industry of employment. Fifty-seven percent of the minority MBAs accepted jobs in manufacturing just after graduation and five years later, 50 percent remained in these industries. Even under the best of circumstances, salaries in manufacturing are smaller than those in management consulting and financial services, industries where white Sloan MBAs worked. Minorities were present in the financial services industry but were more concentrated in commercial banking where the salaries were low in comparison with other private sector industries. The fifth year salary of $44,820 for commercial banking ranked the sixth lowest in eight industry categories.

Although women account for approximately one-third of minority Sloan MBAs, similar to the male-female ratio in the white group, wages of minority women lagged slightly behind those for the minority males and might have reduced the average for the entire minority group. Because fewer minority women attended the Sloan School, the sample of women is small. Of the eight minority women, five lagged behind minority male respondents, and two were at the top level of public sector jobs. Two received wages comparable to males. One did not respond in the fifth year. All of the minority

Table 6-1. Profile of Initial Survey of Minority and White Sloan MBAs, 1975–79 (*percent*).

Descriptor	Minority n = 24	White n = 297
Race		
Black	71	—
White	—	100
Other	29	—
Sex		
Male	67	64
Female	33	36
Type of Program		
Two Year	75	70
AMP	21	27
Five Year (SB/SM)	4	3
Mean Age	27.2 years	27.0 years
Marital Status		
Single	46	54
Married	54	41
Other	—	5
Children		
No children	75	90
Have children	25	10
Undergraduate Major		
Engineering	21	22
Mathematics	21	13
Social Sciences	17	24
Natural Sciences	—	13
Management	21	10
Art/Humanities	12	15
Other	8	2
Undergraduate College		
Quality	58	67
Other	33	30
Foreign	8	3

Table 6-1. continued

Descriptor	Minority n = 24	White n = 297
Sloan Concentration		
Finance	38	39
Organizational Studies	4	7
MIS/Operations Research	29	14
Market/Plan/Control	12	27
Applied Economics	4	2
Industrial Relations	12	3
International Management	—	6
Public Systems	—	2
Mean Years of Prior Full-Time Work Experience	3.2 years	3.2 years
Type of Employer	n = 21[a]	n = 290
Manufacturing	43	27
Management Consulting	9	24
Finance, Real Estate, Insurance	9	7
Public	5	2
High Technology	14	14
Other Services Unknown	—	12
Investment Banking	—	1
Commercial Banking	19	10
Military	—	2
Mean Salary (000)	34.3 ± 8.7	36.1 ± 8.1

a. Three males immediately started graduate school after receiving the degree from the Sloan School.

males also were employed full time at the time of the five-year survey. Three of the group, however, had continued graduate studies on a full-time basis, and their employment at year five represented entry level jobs after three to four years of full time study beyond the Sloan degree.

Between the second and fifth years more minorities had at least one job change (59 percent, versus 36 percent for white MBAs). Table 6-3 shows significant comparisons in this area. These job shifts

Table 6–2. Salaries of Minority MBAs and White MBAs (*adjusted for inflation*).

	Minority MBAs	White MBAs	Minority/White Ratio
Initial Year			
All	$34,322 ± 8.7	$36,149 ± 8.1	94.9%
Manufacturing and High Technology	$35,762	$36,157	98.9%
Year Two			
All	$40,985 ± 8.9	$41,567 ± 10.5	98.6%
Manufacturing and High Technology [a]	$36,067	$41,206	87.5%
Five Year			
All [a]	$44,380 ± 8.4	$50,980 ± 20.2	87.0%
Manufacturing and High Technology	$48,017	$48,311	99.4%

a. Significant difference.

appear to have been lateral moves with no significant increase in salary. It would seem that blacks have traded off salary increases for a perceived, less hostile or more promising workplace. A larger percentage of minorities (43 percent versus 22 percent for whites) indicated that they had lowered their career aspirations, and fewer indicated that they were on track according to the established progression paths of their companies. More minorities saw their companies as setting some constraints on their upward mobility. While most of the white MBAs were employed mainly in the Northeast or on the West Coast, minorities worked in other sections of the country.

Comparing the salaries of minority Sloan MBAs and their white peers in the manufacturing and high technology industries, they were approximately the same in the fifth year—$48,017 and $48,311, respectively. These almost identical salaries obscure a number of important shifts and changes. Minority MBAs who started in manufacturing, particularly in Fortune 500 companies, remained in this industry throughout the five-year period. White MBAs exited from

Table 6–3. Significant Comparisons of Minority and White Sloan
MBAs — Five Years After Graduation (*percent*).

Descriptor	Minority	White[a]
1. Employed in manufacturing	50%	43%
2. Worked on the East or West Coast	39	73
3. One job change since second year survey	59	36
4. Staff positions	71	44
5. Hours/week	54	51
6. Success with respect to own measures or goals	56	72
7. Employer responsible for constraint on progress	53	32
8. Average or moderate job satisfaction	55	26
9. Lowered aspirations	43	22
10. No promotions since last survey	25	18
11. On track according to the established progression paths in their companies	46	58
12. Aggregate salaries (adjusted for inflation)	$44,380	$50,980

a. Includes nine women part-time workers.

management consulting into manufacturing and high technology, but a larger number of white MBAs went to high technology where salaries were slightly below those in manufacturing. Further, a number of the white MBAs reported other benefits in their compensation packages such as stock options and early vesting of pensions. The comparable salaries for minorities and their white Sloan peers do not account for such additional forms of compensation. In conclusion, minority MBAs in manufacturing held their own with reported salaries as compared with their white Sloan counterparts, but did not necessarily keep pace with total compensation.

Chapter 5 noted that women managers experienced considerably more job-related stress than men. because of the small size of the minority Sloan MBA sample, no detailed analysis was made for job-related stress. However, there were several indirect indicators of such stress. After five years, minorities tended to work longer hours per week (fifty-four versus fifty-one) than their Sloan peers. Over half of the minorities reported moderate or average job satisfaction as compared with 26 percent of their classmates who reported in these categories, and nearly three-fifths indicated that they had to modify their behavior in order to fit into the organization. The several individual case studies in this chapter highlight the difficulties of minorities in managerial jobs where negative expectations of their success by peers, subordinates, and especially supervisors remain overwhelming.

Recent research by Bell examines "bicultural stress" and how blacks manage the stresses associated with the movement back and forth between the dominant culture and the black community."[32] The bicultural perspective focuses attention on the interplay between the two cultures and its effect on the lives of minority workers. The minority Sloan MBAs have not reported significant difficulties on this level. With only two exceptions, all had attended predominately white undergraduate schools, had opted to enroll at MIT, and most had some work experience in integrated workplaces. They had good family relations and excellent support systems away from the job. What they described as a critical shortcoming of their workplaces was a scarcity of other black managers with whom they could check out the culture of the company.

Mentoring across racial lines is also important. Fernandez's study of racism and sexism in corporations reported that minority respondents ranked "having a sponsor," as third, behind performance and work experience, as being most advantageous for obtaining desired positions.[33] Approximately two-fifths of the managers in the Fernandez study believed that minorities and women had a more difficult time than did white men in finding someone who was particularly interested in their careers. Thomas's study of the experiences of blacks in gaining mentoring and sponsorship in one large organization concluded that "strong forces mitigate against the formation of cross-racial sponsorship relationships which will be effective at the levels of both the protégés' psychosocial career needs and external career mobility."[34] All of the minority Sloan MBAs who had fewer problems had mentors who were also their supervisors. These MBAs attributed their survival in the early stages of their careers to someone who took a special interest in them. In all cases, the mentor/supervisor initiated the relationship.

CASE STUDIES

In the cases outlined below, five of the most successful males (relative to other minority MBAs), describe the functioning of the internal labor market from the perspective of competent and ambitious minority individuals. At the end of each narrative, the individual responds to a question from the fifth year questionnaire: "How are you perceived by your co-workers?" The narratives are taken verbatim from their responses.

Case A: Black Male, Manufacturing Industry, Line Job in Fifth Year

First Year Survey.   I have not had a rewarding first year as a financial analyst (staff job). I have found more racism and prejudice than anticipated. I expect a new assignment at the end of fifteen months, and this is much slower than my peers. This firm tends to have a "quota" of promotable blacks and that is my major constraint on upward mobility.

Second Year Survey.   I have transferred (not been promoted) to the lowest level in a line management job. I am disappointed in my career path at this time. Although you feel some discrimination in the learning environment (at universities), it is worse in the business environment. My company is reluctant to promote blacks because of the fear of backlash. I am discouraged.

Five-Year Survey.   I have now had two promotions and been rated on my performance appraisal as in the top 5 percent. I am moderately satisfied with my job. The constraint on my progress remains possibly being a black in a very conservative white organization.

Perception of Self by Co-Workers.   Very competitive, hard worker, typical MIT graduate.

Comment.   This Sloan graduate was promoted again within a year after the five-year survey. The slower frequency of promotions for minority MBAs relative to peers in the same workplace may be especially discouraging at the beginning of a professional career. Persistence was eventually rewarded.

Case B: Black Male, Manufacturing Industry, Staff Job, Fifth Year

First Year Survey.   The highlight of my first year was the completion of a major portion of a financial analysis package. The most disappointing was the clash in the management style (Theory X, by control) between my immediate supervisor and me. After nine months, I transferred from this job, which was not challenging, to a job which I enjoy. Just before the lateral transfer (same company), I received a raise. The promotion issue is a big question because the plan is to rotate me to different departments to learn more about the company's operation.

Second Year Survey. I left the (high tech) firm and accepted a job with a manager's title and at a substantial salary increase at this (larger manufacturing) company. I did not seek the position, but was contacted by an executive recruiter, who had received my name from a former supervisor. I am working on the political skills necessary for advancement in a corporation. As a black male, there is the necessity of making the right political moves, particularly with an immediate supervisor. The manner in which the job is done is almost as important as the technical performance.

Five-Year Survey. My compensation is not appropriate for someone with my responsibilities. Two of my subordinates and my predecessor make or earned more than I do. I manage $25 million (after tax) of tax-deferral opportunities. I am pleased with my performance appraisal because it reflects the outstanding work I have done. Because of my technical capabilities, writing skills, and positive attitude, there has been very good acceptance of my abilities. There is no constraint on my progress except an indecision on my part to work at something I truly enjoy (an entrepreneurial activity).

Perception of Self by Co-Workers. Competent, bright, personable, and supportive.

Comment.   This Sloan graduate in his fifth year with the company, has received a 68 percent increase over his entrance salary and now is at the high end of salary for middle managers.

Case C: Black Male, Manufacturing Industry, Staff Job

First Year Survey. Highlights: Top-level exposure within the Division; making presentations to the Vice President and his staff on crucial issues. My job is as challenging as MIT. The planning staff is a small, intense department loaded with MBAs and designated "fast-track" types. I was promoted and received a new job title and salary level.

Second Year Survey. I received two highly effective job performance ratings (second from top category) and a 5 percent merit increase in pay. My ratings place me in the promotable category and three levels of management above me agree that I am ready for promotion. However, my promotion was blocked recently by someone five management levels above me for vague reasons of "seasoning."

Five-Year Survey. I have been promoted into middle management. I am consistently rated superior with an occasional outstanding. I am a trailblazer, following non-traditional routes to upper management. Normal progress is generally much slower. I am a fast tracker, but not a superstar. My last four bosses, all key executives, have served as my mentors and now they are a part of my general network to be called upon as needed, rather than regularly. They have recommended paths to progress and made contacts to facilitate my movement. My next promotion will place me in the bonus eligible category with significantly expanded responsibilities and remuneration. I planned to reach that next level five years out of Sloan. If it takes six or seven years, I will still be happy.

Perception of Self by Co-Workers. Very competent.

Comment. Profiled in a national business journal as one of a new breed of strategic planners.

Case D: Black Male, Financial Services, Staff Job

First Year Survey. A disappointing year mainly because the quantitative training at Sloan School has limited utility in an entry-level management position given the needs of most organizations. I found out what my limitations were and my shortcomings, relative to group dynamics and interaction with other people. I left the major Fortune 500 company after one year to embark on an entrepreneurial career. The company I left was awful, no flexibility with a very tight span of control. Not pleased with performance appraisal. The job was a clerk-like activity.

Second Year Survey. I was recruited by another Fortune 500 company, was promoted and given a larger scope of responsibility. Very satisfied with this job because it has maximum span of control, maximum responsibility, permits creativity, innovation and independence.

Five-Year Survey. Was recruited by another Fortune 500 company as project director and have been promoted to Assistant Vice President, a middle management level. Since I am on the retail side of the house, rather than the institutional side, I am paid moderately lower. It is a function of the industry and not strictly a function of status. I am successful within the conventional measure of job title, status, etc., but I am unsuccessful in accordance with my own internal measures/goals. I would like to be running my own firm. However, I am on the fast track here and am very pleased with my performance appraisal. For the first time, I have a mentor here.

I had some difficulty at my two previous employers because I am aggressive and a risk taker. If you have an aggressive entrepreneurial management style in a conservative company, it won't work. I have had to modify my personal behavior. One of the most significant changes that I have undergone internally is that I no longer pursue the initiative of trying to instill in senior management, a recognition that minorities are under represented. I have tried to transcend the racial and ethnic issues by doing the best job possible.

Perception of Self by Co-Workers.   A rising star.

Comment. Accepted another job in financial services organization after the fifth year survey.

Case E: Black Male, Line Job, Manufacturing

Based on Response in Fifth Year. My progress upward has been slowed because of the deliberate lateral moves I made from manufacturing into marketing. To date, the internal environment has not been conducive to my upward mobility. Movement up is *ad hoc* in general and consequently, there is significant room for exclusion of minorities based on pursely personal breaks.

Some people perceive that I am on a fast track, but I do not believe that I am based on my previous experience, level of current performance, and the position of white males with a similar track record. I have had mentors in the company and have been satisfied with my performance appraisals. My advice to minority MBAs is prepare to work twice as hard as your white peers, then maybe you may attain the same rewards.

Comment. This 1980 graduate from the Sloan School, whose salary has increased by one and one-half times since starting with this company, hopes to reach senior management in two years.

These five success stories are instructive. Four of the individuals were employed in Fortune 500 manufacturing companies. Salaries in manufacturing were lower than those in management consulting or investment banking. The choice of minority MBAs to accept relatively more jobs in manufacturing may have been associated with the fact that many of them were the first ones in their families to become managers in the private sector. Accepting a position with a Fortune 500 company had a particular "halo" effect on the MBAs, that is, one achieved a certain status in accepting a job in those companies. Once hired, minority MBAs might have required more time to find the right fit within the organization. If they were fortunate enough to have a mentor as in Case C, they received the counseling and guidance necessary to function within large bureaucratic structures. If they had several years of comparable work experience in similar environments, as in Case E, they could define for themselves alternative routes or determine whether a shift to a new function would be optimal. If they were without support from supervisors, peers, or mentors, they fought a lonely battle for survival. The Sloan MBA in Case A eventually established an outstanding performance record. If a MBA had a strong propensity to entrepreneurial endeavors, as in Case D, more conservative and status quo-minded management may have forced them to do more than a normal amount of job changing.

The overall salaries of the successful minority Sloan graduates were significantly lower than those of their Sloan peers five years after graduation, but not significantly different from those Sloans who were employed in the manufacturing sector in the fifth year. Since the size of the sample of minority Sloan graduates was small, it was easy to keep in contact with them, by telephone, for some time after the five-year surveys. Several who had hoped to be promoted made the grade in the sixth and seventh year of their post-Sloan work experience. Initially there seemed to be some delay in being promoted, but eventually an outstanding performance record over a longer period was rewarded.

In examining the experience of minority Sloan graduates, there were two issues that did not have parallels among the non-minority Sloans. For some time, practitioners have asserted that minority women may do better than males since they have a double advantage, that is, in affirmative action parlance they provide employers with a "two for" (credit for hiring under both the minority and female goals). The one-third of minority Sloan graduates who were women did not do as well as minority males five years after graduation. Only one was in manufacturing and averaged a salary near the median for the group. Her problems were similar to those described in Chapter 4 on women in manufacturing and after the five-year survey, she transferred to a staff job in the financial services industry. Two of the women were in the public sector at good-paying jobs, but paid below private sector salaries. One had chosen the public sector initially and was pleased with her achievement there. The second had entered the public sector after some major disappointments in a management consulting firm. Four others had started at initial salaries that were below the Sloan average. (As stated previously, one of the minority female MBAs did not respond to the five-year survey.) The women were somewhat younger than their classmates and had little prior work experience. Each had majored in mathematics in undergraduate school and had entered the Sloan program following their graduation from college. Although their salaries had almost doubled over the five-year period, their beginning base pay was low. In the fifth year one was employed in high technology, one in financial services, and two who had moved to small minority-owned consulting firms.

The second issue is frequently discussed as a cultural difference between black managers and white supervisors. A cultural deficit did not appear to be one of the differences that might have shaped their careers. Most of the black managers had attended top quality schools before coming to Sloan and had pursued the same concentrations as their classmates while at Sloan. One respondent noted that he felt no conflict between the corporate culture and his social activities. Having attended an Ivy League school, his leisure-time activities did not seem to differ from those of other Ivy Leaguers. The social requisites of being successful in the private sector certainly embrace social networks, influential family and friends, and few blacks have these even when they have been educated at prestigious schools.

As a group, the minority Sloan MBAs may have been unaware of the gap in salaries between themselves and their Sloan peers. Their measure of job success was whether they were on target with respect to career ladders within their companies. Only 46 percent of the minorities (versus 58 percent of whites) thought they were on track in their companies (see Table 6–3). They worked in places where they rarely encountered other Sloan graduates, and may not have had the information to make the comparison with their Sloan classmates. In their responses to a special questionnaire sent in the Spring of 1986, the minority Sloan graduates indicated that they believed they had done as well as black MBAs from other schools. Even so, only 56 percent (as opposed to 76 percent of their white Sloan peers) felt successful with respect to their work. They somehow felt that they were special. One commented: "As a minority graduate of Sloan School, I feel that it is important to develop linkages with other minority graduates as we progress through our careers. We should be able to provide continuing advice to Sloan, especially on the Sloan curriculum from a minority perspective in business."

Because of the small sample size and complicated story of the minority Sloan MBAs, eight additional Sloans were followed from the classes of 1980 through 1983. They accepted initial employment in the same industries as their classmates. Most entered the financial services industry and five years later have achieved about the same level of job success as their white Sloan counterparts. It is unknown whether this trend will continue for later classes. If the earlier cohorts in the classes of 1975-79 are different, one might speculate that the combination of very aggressive recruiting by Fortune 500 companies for black graduates of leading schools, and the more passive stance of the placement office at the Sloan School in the earlier period, as well as significant changes in the social environment produced a temporary, generational phenomenon of difficulty or lack of success for minority Sloan MBAs.

CONCLUSION

Minority MBAs generally were not as successful as their white Sloan School counterparts when surveyed five years after graduation. As a group, they accepted jobs in manufacturing industries rather than in financial services or management consulting, where the annual salaries and bonuses were higher. Even though reported salaries are the same, when one controls for industry (comparing blacks in manufacturing and high technology with whites in this industry), the compensation packages are different. Black MBAs may earn the same salary but work longer hours per week. Not a single minority male worked in the management consulting industry. Several telephone discussions after the five-year surveys indicated that promotions anticipated by the fifth year were now received. Therefore, the period of demonstrating better than average performance was a longer one for the black MBAs.

These research results are consistent with other research on black managers. Race is still a powerful factor affecting upward mobility in corporate America. This impact will be lessened significantly as more black managers gain experience in a variety of industries and obtain jobs in the private sector. The reassuring finding is that no minority MBA worked in affirmative action or community affairs, jobs which were primary employers of black managers a decade ago. The most discouraging finding was how long some of the minority MBAs floundered before they found an appropriate fit in their first post-management school job; the finding highlights the importance of obtaining more company specific information.

NOTES

1. U.S. Department of Labor, Bureau of Labor Statistics, *Labor Force Statistics Derived From the Current Population Survey: A Databook*, Vol. 1, Bulletin 2096 (Washington, D.C.: U.S. Government Printing Office, September 1982).
2. Ibid.
3. Equal Employment Opportunity Commission, *Equal Employment Opportunity Report, Job Patterns of Minorities and Women in Private Industry* as reported in *Black Enterprise*, March 1987, p. 51.
4. The COGME Schools were: Harvard University, Columbia University, Massachusetts Institute of Technology (Alfred P. Sloan School of Management), Dartmouth College (Amos Tuck School of Business Administration), University of Chicago, University of Pennsylvania (Wharton School), Stanford University, Carnegie-Mellon University, University of California at Berkeley, and Cornell University.
5. The Consortium Program for Graduates in Management was started in 1966 and included the University of Wisconsin, Indiana University, Washington University at St. Louis, University of North Carolina at Chapel Hill, University of Southern California, and the University of Rochester.
6. U.S. Department of Labor, *A Study of Black Male Professionals In Industry* Manpower Research, Monograph No. 26 (Washington, D.C.: U.S. Government Printing Office, 1973).
7. Ibid., p. 2.
8. John P. Fernandez, *Black Managers in White Corporations* (New York: John Wiley and Sons, 1975).
9. Ibid., p. 78.
10. Ibid., p. 140.
11. Ibid., p. 201.
12. Harold Brown and David L. Ford, "An Exploratory Analysis of Discrimination in the Employment of Black MBA Graduates," *Journal of Applied Psychology* 62 (1977): 50–56.

13. Richard America and Bernard Anderson, *Moving Ahead: Black Managers in American Business* (New York: McGraw-Hill, 1978).

14. Heidrick and Struggles, Inc., *Profiles of Black Executives* (Chicago: Heidrick and Struggles, Inc., 1979).

15. Ibid., pp. 1–8.

16. C.P. Alderfer, C.J. Alderfer, L. Tucker, and R. Tucker, "Diagnosing Race Relations in Management," *Journal of Applied Behavioral Science* 16 (June 1980): 135–66.

17. Ibid., p. 148.

18. Ibid., pp. 149–50.

19. Ibid., pp. 152–53.

20. John P. Fernandez, *Racism and Sexism in Corporate Life: Changing Values in American Business* (Lexington, Mass.: Lexington Books, 1981).

21. Ibid., p. 119.

22. Ibid., p. 53.

23. Ibid., p. 57.

24. Ibid., pps. 106, 211, 214.

25. Arthur Beaty, Jr., and O. Lester Smithers, Jr., "Comparative Analysis of Career Anchors of Black Professional and Managers in the Private and Public Sectors," Master's thesis, Sloan School of Management at MIT, 1985.

26. Edgar H. Schein, *Career Dynamics: Matching Individual and Organizational Needs* (Reading, Mass.: Addison-Wesley Publishing Co., 1978), pp. 124–46.

27. David A. Thomas and Clayton P. Alderfer, "The Influence of Race on Career Dynamics: Theory and Research on Minority Career Experiences," in M.B. Arthur, D.T. Hall, and B.S. Lawrence, ed., *Handbook of Career Theory*, Cambridge University Press (in press).

28. Ibid.

29. Ibid.

30. Edward W. Jones, "What It's Like to be a Black Manager," *Harvard Business Review* (July/August 1973): 108–16.

31. Edward W. Jones, "Black Managers: The Dream Deferred," *Harvard Business Review* (May/June 1986): 84–93.

32. E.L. Bell, "The Power Within: Bicultural Life Structures and Stress Among Black Women" (Ph.D. dissertation, Case Western Reserve, 1986).

33. Fernandez, *Racism and Sexism*, p. 134.

34. David A. Thomas, "Black Experiences of Gaining Mentoring and Sponsorship in Organizations (Presented at the Academy of Management 1987 Annual Meeting, New Orleans, Louisiana, June 24, 1987).

7 CONCLUSIONS

What is the significance of this research for MBAs, employers, and schools of business and management? This text has examined the post-management school experience of a select group of MBAs five years into their careers. MBAs still do not comprise a majority of individuals who enter management in both the private and public sectors. The typical developmental pattern has been learning on the job and promotion from within. Lateral entry at senior management levels is not the standard procedure for the corporate hierarchy or for even flatter organizational structures. However, MBAs, especially those in this study, are perceived and treated as fast trackers and attain the upper levels of middle management in a shorter period of time.

To reiterate the major findings:

1. Industry of employment is the most significant determinant of MBA compensation five years after graduation from management school.

2. For male MBAs, in addition to the industry variables, work experience prior to attendance at management school, travel time, and mentoring were significant. For female MBAs, in addition to industry, only the hours per week appeared to be significant determinants of fifth year compensation.

149

3. Sloan women MBAs endured greater hardships in order to attain the equivalent compensation and rewards of their Sloan male peers. The higher psychic costs were significantly more job-related stress, more hours per week in the entry years of their careers, more difficulties with mentoring relationships, the hardship of searching for quality child care, the necessity of giving up full-time careers for part-time arrangements, and more problems in integrating their work and non-work activities. Some of these psychic costs are imposed by the social environment. Only after internalizing most of these externalities ascribed to them can Sloan women MBAs earn the same salary as men.

4. Minority MBAs were not as successful as their white Sloan peers even after one controls for industry of employment. Although reported salaries in the manufacturing industries (where minorities clustered) appeared to be comparable to salaries paid to whites in these industries, the compensation packages differed. Minority MBAs did not work in management consulting and financial consulting, where their white Sloan peers were employed. The minority MBAs had to wait longer for promotions, worked longer hours, and floundered more at the beginning of their post-management schools careers.

In the remainder of this chapter, Sloan MBA fifth year salaries, future prospects for women and minority MBAs, and implications of the findings for employers and management schools will be briefly reviewed.

FIFTH YEAR SALARIES

Within the MBA category, individuals may have some initial differential advantages in compensation that are associated with the standing of their schools. These assessments, based on the ratings of the deans of Schools of Management, industry recruiters, or alumni/ae, place the Sloan School at MIT among the country's top five graduate schools of management. MBAs are a special group within management, and MBAs from the leading schools may have higher initial salaries, receive more selective grooming for more responsible jobs, and may be designated earlier as those with high potential for senior management.[1] One finding from the research is that (except for pub-

Table 7-1. Percentage Increase in Salary by Year Five by Sloan School Concentration.

Concentration	Percent of Initial Respondents (n = 319)	Percent Salary Increases by Year Five
Finance	38	64
MIS/Operation Research	15	43
Planning/Control	26	57
International Management	6	43
Industrial Relations	4	59
Organizational Studies[a]	7	63
Applied Economics	2	29
Public Systems	2	45
	Overall Salary	56

a. Includes what is now called Management of Technology.

lic systems as an area of concentration) most Sloan MBAs were well compensated by the fifth year after graduation.

Initial salaries for graduates in all concentrations in management school (excluding public systems) ranged from $31,000 to $34,640 (adjusted for inflation). Eighty percent of the Sloan MBAs had concentrated in three fields: finance, management information systems, and planning and control. By the fifth year Sloans in each field had significant increases in salaries. Even for areas with a smaller percentage of graduates, the percent increases in salaries were high. (See Table 7-1.) Regardless of the area of concentration while in management school, Sloan MBAs performed well. In Chapter 3 such mobility indicators as change of functions, promotions, and change of employers were discussed, and in Chapter 4, the impact of industry migrations. These exits and entries into industries shaped the economic outcomes of the Sloan MBAs.

Another way of viewing the importance of industry of employment is through an examination of salaries of finance majors by industry of employment in the fifth year as shown in Table 7-2. It is clear that the controlling variable is industry. The Sloan MBAs were graduated between 1975 and 1979 and represented the post-Vietnam War baby boomers. Males were mostly successful in their professional and personal lives. The few who experienced temporary unemploy-

Table 7-2. Finance Majors by Industry of Employment in the Fifth Year.

Industry	Average Salary (Constant dollars)
Manufacturing	$46,360
High Technology	46,080
Finance, real estate, insurance[a]	73,950
Management consulting	58,650
Public sector	50,560
Other services	47,220
Commercial banking	47,690
Finance Majors	$54,530
Male	54,940
Female	53,800
Total MBAs (all areas)	*$51,230*

a. Includes investment banking.

ment quickly found new positions. The propensity to work in small-scale organizations rather than in corporate hierarchies, as well as a strong entrepreneurial bent, produced young managers who felt more comfortable in more unstructured work environments.

PROSPECTS FOR WOMEN AND MINORITY MBAs

Women MBAs, as newcomers in management, did as well in monetary terms, but the psychic costs of success were higher than for males. By the second year women worked, on the average, a significantly larger number of hours per week and expressed their anxiety of living up to a standard of excellence set for women managers as a group. In a variety of ways, employers implied that these women would be judged not only on their individual performance but also would have to prove that they did not fit a stereotype of women workers with short-term interests in their jobs. Overcoming these hurdles took its psychological toll, and some of the women respondents indicated extreme fatigue and exhaustion. Since nearly all of the women were partners in dual career relationships, they had many concerns about meshing their professional and personal lives. A few, in their single-minded pursuit of careers, sacrificed their marriages and personal relationships.

The five-year surveys were completed before many of the women had decided how to engage in a full-time career and at the same time to have children. They discussed what they perceived as a traumatic decision to be made in the near future. If they postponed having children until their late thirties, many would have at least a decade of solid work experience. On the other hand, if they started a family sooner, they spoke reluctantly of settling for a less challenging full-time position or a part-time work experience that might not enhance their careers.

While the future for these women Sloan MBAs might appear dimmer than their trailblazing first five years, the minority Sloan MBAs have yet to catch up with their Sloan peers. For those who started their managerial careers in the manufacturing industries, the lag can be attributed to choice of industry. After overcoming the initial problems of slower promotions, the minority Sloans may reach a plateau within these corporate structures. The difficulty of career movements, as well as the likelihood of corporate restructuring and reduction of the managerial work force, are dual threats. Black managers may have greater difficulty finding comparable positions if they are caught in restructuring or staff reductions. There has been some concern recently about how the perceived lag in post-graduate career advancement could have negative consequences for minority enrollment in graduate business schools.[2]

The Sloan MBAs are representative of their MBA population, but the issues they faced were quite different from those faced by the successful senior mangers of today. The Bureau of Labor Statistics has projected a 29 percent increase in their occupational category—executive, administrative and managerial workers between 1986 and the year 2000. Approximately 14 million managers will account for 10 percent of civilian employment.[3] If MBAs increase their share of managerial jobs, as seems probable, women and minority males will maintain their presence there. However, it is likely by the year 2000 that there will be significant changes in the nature and types of managerial tasks. More researchers have provided insights on the impact of information technology. Organizations of the future may well be networks in which hierarchies are not important.[4] Sloan MBAs, in this research, were forerunners of managers who will operate on a team or in a highly unstructured environment. As noted earlier, MBAs who worked in management consulting and in some areas of financial services operated on a project basis as a member of a team. Responsibility was rotated so that an individual might serve as team leader on one project and a resource person on the next.

Although the emphasis had been on compensation as the measure of career success, the Sloan women MBAs started to shift away from this norm at the end of five years. They weighted their priorities on the side of family issues and work that made a contribution to society. More women worked in nonprofit organizations. Some quality-of-work concerns were also articulated by those males who had left large corporations to work in smaller companies. The work was seen as more challenging and as providing more autonomy. This preference for small-size firms and entrepreneurial ventures might enable Sloan MBAs to adapt to the shrinking opportunities in middle management as these positions are reduced in larger firms. Mergers, acquisions, divestitures, "downsizing," other types of corporate restructuring, and global competition will continue to transform the nature of managerial work.

IMPLICATIONS FOR MANAGEMENT SCHOOLS AND EMPLOYERS

As this book was being finished, the new dean of the Sloan School formulated a new mission that would focus on the "development and dissemination of knowledge for improving management in the context of a global economy with increasing technological competition and the need for more rapid organizational change." While there may be significant modifications in the curriculum to incorporate these dimensions, the core curriculum, as in the past, will provide the foundation for the Master's Program. The respondents to the survey generally believed that the cool, analytical style of their Sloan management education had been a big plus in their careers. Some considered effective communication of ideas a shortcoming when they responded to the five-year survey (years 1980 through 1984). No courses were offered then on verbal and written communications—one male engineer who responded wrote "make the engineers talk!" Today a communications program is fully integrated into the curriculum. In the future it might prove useful to have graduates assess the relevance of their management education to their world of work.

This ten-year span (1975–84) of research underscores the fact that employers may not fully comprehend the consequences of the revolutionary changes in the composition of the U.S. labor market. Since 1983, white males no longer made up the majority of the country's civilian labor force. In 1986, women and minority males comprised 56 percent of the civilian labor force. The U.S. Bureau of Labor Statistics projects that between the years 1986 and 2000, women will account for 63 percent of all of the new workers entering the labor market. Thus, some of the key dilemmas of interaction of work and the family will have to be resolved. The Sloan women MBAs represented the brightest and the best, and if they experienced difficulties in jobs for which they were very well qualified, one wonders about the chances of other women workers achieving equity in the workplace.

Many private sector employers, in order to attract and retain a productive work force, have added family-oriented benefit programs such as "flex-time" work schedules, parental leave, and job sharing. Child care, another family benefit, was a central issue in the presidential campaign of 1988 as both parties sought the votes of working mothers. These non-salary benefits are seen as reducing absenteeism and turnover. One large pharmaceutical company has calculated the savings of family-oriented programs and notes that "even after the cost of the leave policy for child care is deducted, it adds an average pretax value of $12,000 an employee, since the company saves the expense of training new workers."[5]

To the extent that minority MBAs found their upward mobility into senior management unfairly blocked, this sends a signal to a much larger group of workers that investment in human capital may have a limited payoff. Employers have responded to both women and minorities by improving their performance measurements, expanding opportunities for development, treating dual career couples not as deviants, and evaluating and modifying relocation procedures for managerial workers. Much of the focus had been on corporate hierarchies and perhaps, as the workplaces change, the options available to employers will be increased.

FUTURE RESEARCH

In the initial years of their careers, Sloan MBAs obtained good jobs, advanced rapidly, and were generally satisfied with their progress. But within the first five years, signs of stress also begin to appear. Some of the women graduates opted out of the standard career route by shifting to part-time positions in order to care for children. Others, both men and women, began to report that the dual career family—in which many participated—though a source of support, occasionally produced much stress and tension, particularly when geographic mobility was required for career advancement. A follow-up study of these young managers would enhance our knowledge about the variety of managerial careers and the particular characteristics associated with each industry. Management consulting was the initial choice of MBAs in the late 1970s, and investment banking and other financial services fulfilled this role in the 1980s. Will management of technology represent their industry of choice in the 1990?

A follow-up study of the original cohort of women might center on the concern for having and caring for children. During the next five years many felt that they may hit the "glass ceiling" and may decide to become entrepreneurs or search in other directions for the optimum mix of professional and personal achievement. One Sloan woman MBA who continued discussions with the author beyond the five-year period followed a career trajectory that may reveal many of the problems that women managers face in non-traditional assignments. A fast tracker in the manufacturing sector, she had considerable geographic mobility; achieved job success at year five with significant job-related stress; put her personal life "on hold" while her professional track record was established; reached, in her terms, the "big three-0," with some anxiety; turned down a challenging, major new job to marry, have a child, and retreat to a small town; and lastly, decided, with a dual career spouse, to be an entrepreneurial team.

Although minority Sloan MBAs, especially black males, started to pursue similar employment opportunities—as did their white peers in the 1980s—will the outcome of delayed promotions and less-than-satisfying jobs continue, as with the minorities in earlier Sloan classes? Will the upward mobility of other non-white males, primarily Asians, help black males? In a survey of sixty-six Asian American graduates from the Master's Program at the Sloan School, Bay found that almost three-fourths believed that Asian Americans were underrepresented in top management. However, they expected to attain senior management as they gained more seniority.[6] This book ends with guarded optimism that some women and minority males will become a visible presence in the ranks of American managers. That is progress compared to a decade ago.

NOTES

1. "Remaking the Harvard B-School." *Business Week*, March 24, 1986.
2. "Business Schools Cautioned on Minority Role," *The New York Times*, December 13, 1987.
3. U.S. Bureau of Labor Statistics, *Monthly Labor Review* (Washington, D.C.: U.S. Government Printing Office, September 1987), p. 51.
4. Edgar Schein, "Is There A Future for Manager Development? An Examination Of The Divine Right Of Managers." (Presented to University Executive Program, Director's International Conference, Litchfield Park, Arizona, April 1988.)
5. Glenn Collins, "Wooing Workers in the 90's: New Role for Family Benefits," *The New York Times*, July 20, 1988.
6. John C. Bay, "Determinants Of The Upward Mobility of Asian Americans In General Management," Master's thesis, Sloan School of Management at MIT, May 1987.

APPENDIXES

APPENDIX A

Five-Year Status, Sloan MBAs, Employed Full Time.[a]

Variable	Women	% of Female Respondents	Men	% of Male Respondents
Total	67	34[b]	128	66[b]
1. Industry	67	100	128	100
Manufacturing	12	18	34	27
High technology	13	19	30	23
Finance, Insurance, Real Estate (FIRE)	3	5	12	9
Management consulting	14	21	22	17
Public sector	3	5	5	4
Other services	14	21	12	9
Investment banking	1	1	4	3
Commercial banking	7	10	7	6
Military	–	–	2	2
2. Changed employers during past three years	66	100	127	100
None	29	44	73	58
One or more	37	56	54	42
3. Changed functions during past three years (yes)	31	48	57	45
4. Number of promotions since last survey	52	100	112	100
None	7	10	22	20
One or more	45	90	90	80

5. Job classification	_67_	_100_	_126_	_100_
Staff	21	31	35	28
Line	13	19	32	25
Staff/line	14	21	25	20
Consultant	12	18	18	14
Entrepreneur and self-employed	6	9	15	12
Other	1	2	1	1
6. Average number of employees in firm	200	—	200	—
7. Position in hierarchy	_62_	_100_	_121_	_100_
Junior management	13	21	37	30
Middle management	36	58	60	50
Senior management	13	21	24	20
8. Level commensurate with qualifications (yes)	53	83	92	78
9. Title appropriate for responsibilities (yes)	48	75	100	84
10. Compensation appropriate for level (yes)	45	71	88	75
11. People supervised	_49_	_100_	_83_	_100_
None	10	20	15	18
1–5	17	35	31	37
6–10	3	6	9	11
11–20	5	10	8	10
20 plus	9	19	15	18
Varies	5	10	5	6
12. Job security	_64_	_100_	_124_	_100_
Poor	7	11	7	5
Good	20	31	58	47
Excellent	37	58	59	48

(Appendix A. continued overleaf)

Appendix A. continued

Variable	Women	% of Female Respondents 34[b]	Men	% of Male Respondents 66[b]
Total	*67*		*128*	
13. Percentage of time/travel	66	100	120	100
None	21	32	35	29
1–10 percent	23	35	34	28
11–25 percent	8	12	21	18
26–60 percent	9	14	21	18
Above 60 percent	1	1	6	5
Varies	4	6	3	2
14. Hours worked per week				
Mean	52.1 (±7.0)			52.3 (±10.0)
15. Hours/week as norm for firm	62	100	119	100
Standard	38	61	66	56
High for firm	24	39	48	40
Low for firm	–	–	5	4
16. Mean salary (adjusted for inflation	$49,580 (±16.7)		$52,100 (±20.0)	
17. Compensation include bonus (yes)	9	13	31	24
18. Bonus—Mean	$6,509		$17,294	
19. Success with respect to measure of your organization (yes)	47	83	86	81
20. Success with respect to own measure (yes)	50	77	86	72

21.	On track according to progression path (yes)	26	54	49	61
22.	On track according to personal potential (yes)	29	69	62	64
23.	Constraints on progress	60	100	111	100
	Self	25	42	45	41
	Company	23	38	37	33
	Environment	5	8	14	13
	None	7	12	15	13
24.	Job satisfaction	65	100	126	100
	Dissatisfied	3	5	9	7
	Moderately satisfied	6	9	17	14
	Average satisfied	12	18	20	16
	Above average	30	46	38	30
	Very satisfied	14	22	42	33
25.	Satisfied with performance appraisal (yes)	45	90	68	71
26.	Job credibility problems	65	100	118	100
	yes	17	26	22	19
	no	28	43	76	64
	Initial problems	20	31	20	17
27.	Supportive co-workers (yes)	54	86	97	84
28.	Competitive co-workers (yes)	44	70	77	67
29.	Sex of co-workers	64	100	114	100
	Female	5	8	6	5
	Male	50	78	93	82
	50/50	6	9	14	12
	Varies	3	5	1	1

(Appendix A. continued overleaf)

Appendix A. continued

Variable	Total	Women	% of Female Respondents	Men	% of Male Respondents
		67	34[b]	128	66[b]
30. Supportive supervisor (yes)		56	93	91	85
31. Competent supervisor (yes)		50	83	92	84
32. Sex of supervisor		63	100	109	100
Female		8	13	4	4
Male		53	84	105	96
Varies		2	3	—	—
33. Perception of self by peers—coincides with own self-image (yes)		50	82	94	90
34. Modify behavior to fit organization		59	100	106	100
Some		41	69	44	41
Very little		11	19	39	37
None		7	12	23	22
35. Is dress important?		67	100	124	100
Very		28	42	44	35
Somewhat		28	42	52	42
Not at all		11	16	28	23
36. Left work force (yes)		15	23	14	11
37. Career aspirations changed (yes)		38	58	58	47

38. Changed aspirations	*31*	*100*	*45*	*100*
Lowered	9	29	6	13
Increased	8	26	2	5
Became entrepreneur	5	16	6	13
More defined	9	29	31	69
Mentors (Variables 39–53)				
39. Mentor	*64*	*100*	*118*	*100*
Yes/positive experience	35	55	50	42
Yes/negative experience	6	9	3	3
No mentor	23	36	65	55
40. Mentor's place in the organization	*32*	*100*	*45*	*100*
Senior management	17	53	20	45
Supervisor	7	22	13	29
Middle management	5	16	6	13
Outside organization	3	9	2	4
Relative	—	—	1	2
Other	—	—	3	7
41. Length of time your mentor served (average year)	2.4 years		2.8 years	
42. Age difference	*32*	*100*	*46*	*100*
Significantly older	20	63	31	67
Significantly younger	1	3	—	—
No difference	11	34	15	33
43. Number of years difference in age	12.8 years		12.5 years	

(Appendix A. continued overleaf)

Appendix A. continued

Variable	Women	% of Female Respondents	Men	% of Male Respondents
Total	67	34[b]	128	66[b]
44. Have you had a mentor in the past? (yes)	23	64	28	61
45. Have you served as mentor?	62	100	107	100
Yes	30	48	44	41
No	32	52	63	59
46. Does mentor provide sponsorship?	27	100	36	100
Yes	7	26	5	14
No	20	74	31	86
47. Does mentor provide exposure/visibility?	27	100	36	100
Yes	4	15	6	17
No/not mentioned	23	85	30	83
48. Does mentor provide coaching, give advice?	27	100	36	100
Yes	26	96	32	89
No/not mentioned	1	4	4	11
49. Does mentor provide protection, support?	27	100	36	100
Yes	3	11	4	11
No/not mentioned	24	89	32	89
50. Does mentor provide challenging assignments?	27	100	36	100
Yes	2	7	2	6
No/not mentioned	25	93	34	94

51. Does mentor provide acceptance?	*27*	*100*	*36*	*100*
Yes	–	–	1	3
No/not mentioned	27	100	35	97
52. Does mentor provide counseling on a personal level?	*27*	*100*	*36*	*100*
Yes	1	4	2	6
No/not mentioned	26	96	34	94
53. Does mentor provide friendship?	*27*	*100*	*36*	*100*
Yes	–	–	1	3
No/not mentioned	27	100	35	97
Stress (Variables 54–57)				
54. Stress in worklife (scaled intensity, 1–5)	*65*	*100*	*121*	*100*
1) No stress	9	14	34	28
2)	16	24	36	30
3)	20	31	37	30
4)	9	14	8	7
5) Lots of stress	11	17	6	5
55. Stress	*56*	*100*	*85*	*100*
Caused by work	52	93	80	94
Caused by personal life	4	7	5	6
56. Stress affects work	*54*	*100*	*84*	*100*
Helps	5	9	5	6
Hurts	23	43	43	51
No effect	26	48	36	43

(Appendix A. continued overleaf)

Appendix A. continued

Variable	Total	Women 67	% of Female Respondents 34[b]	Men 128	% of Male Respondents 66[b]
57. Coping with stress		_56_	_100_	_80_	_100_
Outside		5	9	–	–
Self-help		40	71	55	69
No effective way		11	20	25	31
Personal Life (Variables 58–73)					
58. Marital status		_66_	_100_	_126_	_100_
Married		38	58	81	64
Not married		21	32	36	29
Divorced/separated		7	10	9	7
59. Have children (yes)		16	32	47	50
60. Child-care arrangements		_13_	_100_	_46_	_100_
Spouse at home		1	8	32	70
Sitter		6	46	2	4
Day-care		3	23	3	6
School		2	15	5	11
Other/combinations		1	8	4	9
61. Childcare satisfactory (yes)		11	92	39	95
62. Hours spent with children during work week		3.0 hr/wk (av)		2.3 hr/wk (av)	

63. Dual career marriage (yes)	39	91	39	43
64. Spouse's career affects relationship	32	100	42	100
Problems/constraints	8	25	13	31
No problems/no effects	13	41	15	36
Helps	11	34	14	33
65. Progress of spouse's career	36	100	49	100
As far	19	53	13	27
Further	10	28	5	10
Not as far	7	19	31	63
66. Your career affects relationship	36	100	46	100
Problems	10	28	17	37
No problems	6	17	15	33
Helps	20	55	14	30
67. Spouse career/your career	36	100	49	100
Constraints	13	36	12	24
No effect	7	20	22	45
Helps	16	44	15	31
68. Household duties done	61	100	116	100
Self	23	38	31	27
Shared	21	34	38	33
Spouse	3	5	40	34
Other	14	23	7	6
69. Stress at home	37	100	45	100
Caused by work	30	81	37	82
Caused by personal life	7	19	8	18

(Appendix A. continued overleaf)

Appendix A. continued

Variable	Women	% of Female Respondents	Men	% of Male Respondents
Total	67	34[b]	128	66[b]
70. Job/personal life interfere	65	100	121	100
A lot	16	25	38	31
Some	22	34	38	31
Not much	19	29	37	31
None	8	12	8	7
71. Significant change in personal life (yes)	39	62	65	53
72. Satisfied with balance work/non-work (yes)	35	54	73	58
73. Most supportive to help deal with problems	67	100	123	100
Spouse	31	47	67	55
Friend	26	39	23	19
Peers	2	3	3	2
Parents	1	1	5	4
Other	6	9	15	12
No support	1	1	4	3
Self	—	—	6	5
74. Entrepreneurs	67	100	128	100
No	47	70	74	58
Yes, family owned	2	3	5	4
Yes, self-owned	6	9	15	12
Has considered	12	18	34	26

a.   Percentages pertain to individuals responding to the specific question. See questionnaire for Fifth Year Survey in Appendix B.

APPENDIX B

Initial, Second, and Five-Year Survey:
Graduates from the Sloan School Master's Program

Initial Survey:
Graduates From the Sloan School Master's Program

NAME:
(*Note: Use your ID number if*
you prefer not to use your name.) _____

IDENTIFICATION ≠ : _____

HOME ADDRESS: _____

_____

AGE: _____

MARITAL STATUS:	*NUMBER OF DEPENDENTS:*
Single ☐	Children _____
Married ☐	Spouse _____
Divorced ☐	Others _____
Separated ☐	

EDUCATION:

Undergraduate School: _____

Year Graduated _____ Major _____

Sloan School Experience:

Concentration _____

Thesis Topic _____

Other Graduate School: _____

Year Graduated _____ Field _____

WORK EXPERIENCE: (*prior to Sloan School*)

	Job Title	Number of Years
Full Time	_____	_____
Part Time	_____	_____
Summer	_____	_____

JOB ACCEPTED AS OF JUNE:

Job Title _____

Company _____

Salary _____ Location _____

Initial Survey:
Graduates From the Sloan School Master's Program

(1) Do you plan routine and regular participation in the labor force over the next 10 years? _____

(2) What are your career objectives?

_____

_____

_____

(3) What kind of job do you think that you will have by the end of the next five years? ten years? (Give both salary and job titles.)

_____

_____

_____

(4) If you are married,

    (a) What is your spouse's profession? _____

    (b) Are you planning to work and live in a city other than the one where your spouse works or lives? _____

Additional Comments:

(Appendix B. continued overleaf)

Second Year Follow-up—June:
Graduates From the Sloan School Master's Program

NAME:
(*Note: Use your ID number if*
you prefer not to use your name.) _____

IDENTIFICATION ≠:   _____

I. *JOB HISTORY*

1. What is your present job title? _____

2. Name of employer _____

3. Number of employees in your:

    a. Company _____ b. Plant _____ c. Unit _____

4. Is your job the same one noted on your response to the June _____
   questionnaire?

    Yes ☐ (Proceed to Question 6)

    No ☐ (Proceed to Question 5)

5. How has your job changed? (Describe)

    _____

    _____

    a. Promotion/same company _____

    b. Transfer/same company (lateral move) _____

    c. Changed employers _____

    d. Other _____

6. On your present job:

    a. Describe duties _____

    b. Actual hours worked per week (include formal/homework/overtime)

    _____

    c. Are you in staff or line? _____

7. Have you received any special commendations, bonuses, rewards?
   Discuss.

    _____

8. What kinds of skills do you need for your job? _____

    _____

Second Year Follow-up—June:
Graduates From the Sloan School Master's Program

9. Do you lack any skill that you think might further enhance your career?

   No ☐

   Yes ☐ Discuss _____

10. What kinds of on-the-job training have you had?

    a. *Formal Courses*   *Duration*

       Internal

       External

    b. *Informal Assistance*   *Describe*

       Supervisor

       Mentor

       Colleagues

       Others

11. If you have not been promoted, do you expect to be promoted soon?

    Yes ☐

    No ☐

    Why not? _____

12. Compensation per annum _____

13. Have you made any geographic shifts?

    Yes ☐   Where? _____

    No ☐

14. a. What have been the most rewarding elements of your experience as a manager? _____

    b. The most disappointing aspects? _____

15. Are you satisfied with your present job?

    Yes ☐ (Proceed to Question 16)

    No ☐ Why not? _____

(Appendix B. continued overleaf)

Second Year Follow-up—June:
Graduates From the Sloan School Master's Program

---

16. Check one for your job satisfaction:
    1. Dissatisfied ☐   2. Moderately satisfied ☐
    3. Average satisfaction ☐ 4. Very satisfied ☐

17. How do you get along with your subordinates?
    1. Do not ☐   2. Fair ☐
    3. Average ☐   4. Very well ☐

18. How would you rate your productivity relative to your peers?
    1. Low ☐   2. Average ☐
    3. High ☐   4. Exceptional ☐

19. Describe briefly your relationship with your *immediate* supervisor.

    _____

20. Were you pleased with your performance appraisal?

    _____

21. Did your supervisor indicate shortcomings, strengths, offer advice?
    Yes ☐
    No ☐
    Explain. _____

22. Are you on the career path that you envisioned when you left Sloan School?
    Yes ☐
    No ☐
    Explain. _____

23. Have you had to cope with problems on the job that you had not anticipated when you graduated from Sloan School? If yes, explain.

    _____

II. *NON-WORK ACTIVITIES*

24. Any significant changes in your personal life?
    Marital Status ☐   Children ☐
    Other dependents ☐   Health ☐
    Other ☐

Second Year Follow-up—June:
Graduates From the Sloan School Master's Program

---

25. How have you integrated your work and non-work activities?

    No problems   ☐

    Some problems   ☐

    Describe: _____

    Many problems   ☐

    Describe: _____

26. What effect (if any) has your job had on your activities away from work?

    _____

27. What effect (if any) has your life away from work had on your job?

    _____

28. Do you travel more than 5 miles to work?

    Yes ☐   Mode: _____

    No   ☐

29. Do you like the community in which you live?

    Yes ☐   No ☐

30. Does your job require travel?

    Frequently   ☐   Average   ☐

    Infrequently ☐

Additional Comments:

(Appendix B. continued overleaf)

Five-Year Follow-up Survey:
Sloan School Class of

NAME:
(Note: Use your ID number if
you prefer not to use your name.) _____

EMPLOYER: _____

TOTAL NUMBER OF EMPLOYEES: _____

GEOGRAPHIC LOCATION: _____

DEPARTMENT: _____

JOB TITLE: _____

If you are an entrepreneur or working in a family-owned business please so specify and answer as many questions as applicable.

Entrepreneur   Yes ☐   No ☐ Please see Question 58.

1. Have you changed employers in the past 3 years?   Yes ☐ No ☐

   If yes, please give name of former employer, dates of changes and reason for changing employers.

2. Have you changed functions (fields) in the last 3 years? Yes ☐ No ☐

   If yes, please list former function, date of change and reason for changing functions.

3. Have you been promoted in the last 3 years?   Yes ☐ No ☐

   If yes,
   Numbers of Promotions _____

   Dates of Promotions _____

   If not promoted, why not? _____

4. Are you if staff, line, or staff with line responsibility?
   Staff   ☐   Line   ☐
   Staff/Line Responsibility ☐   Consultant   ☐

5. What is the hierarchy in your organization? Please specify your position in this hierarchy. _____

   Junior Management   ☐   Middle Management ☐
   Senior Management   ☐

6. Define the middle management for your company.

Five-Year Follow-up Survey
Sloan School Class of

7. Do you have exposure to top management in your firm? Yes ☐   No ☐
   If yes, how is this exposure provided?

Job reporting layer	☐	Mentor facilitation	☐
Project basis	☐	Other (Please specify)	☐ _____

8. Is your firm innovative or conservative in nature (i.e., is the management in your firm willing to try new approaches to doing business and solving problems)?

   Yes ☐   No ☐

9. Is your firm generally competitive or cooperative internally (i.e., does the firm emphasize high mobility)?

   Competitive ☐   Cooperative ☐

   Other ☐ _____

10. Please give your job description for your current job.

   _____

11. Are you at an organization level commensurate with your training and work experience to date?   Yes ☐   No ☐

12. (a) Do you feel that your job title is appropriate for someone with your responsibilities?   Yes ☐   No ☐
       If no, explain. _____

   (b) Do you feel that your compensation is appropriate for someone with your responsibilities? Yes ☐   No ☐
       If no, explain. _____

13. How would you rate your job security?
    Poor ☐   Good ☐   Excellent ☐

14. How much travel is required in your job? _____

15. How many hours (on average) do you work per week? _____
    Is this standard for your firm? _____

16. What is your current salary? (Please specify range if you do not wish to give an exact figure.) Does this include bonus?   Yes ☐   No ☐

17. Have there been any major reorganizations or mergers in your firm since you have been employed there?   Yes ☐   No ☐
    Did the organization organization or merger affect your job?
    Please explain. _____

(Appendix B. continued overleaf)

Five-Year Follow-up Survey
Sloan School Class of

18. How is "success" measured in your organization/department? _____
    (a) Have you been successful with respect to these measures?
        Please explain. _____
    (b) Have you been successful with respect to your own measures or goals?
        Please explain. _____

19. (a) Is there a usual progression path for those in your position?
        Please explain. _____
    (b) Above entry level jobs, does your company bring in people laterally
        from the outside? _____
    (c) What is the time frame for this progression? _____
    (d) Are you on track according to this framework? _____
    (e) Are you on track according to your potential? Please explain.
        _____

20. What are the constraints on your progress? _____

21. What are the drivers/facilitators of your progress? Please explain.
    _____

22. Do you have expertise in a technical field?   Yes ☐   No ☐
    If yes, does your work emphasize this technical expertise or your MBA
    skills? Is this emphasis based on your own preferences? Please explain.
    _____

23. Do you have (or have you had) supervisory responsibility?   Yes ☐   No ☐
    If yes, how many people did you supervise? _____
    Length of supervision? _____
    What were the rewarding aspects? _____
    What were the disappointing aspects? _____

24. Please rate your job satisfaction: (1–5 is low to high).
    1. Dissatisfied   ☐   2. Moderately satisfied   ☐
    3. Average Satisfaction ☐   4. Above Average   ☐
    5. Very Satisfied   ☐
    If not very satisfied, is there anything that you would change that would
    improve your satisfaction ? _____

Five-Year Follow-up Survey
Sloan School Class of

25. Were you pleased with your performance appraisals? Please explain.

26. Have you had any problems gaining or maintaining credibility in the performance of your job? _____

27. Are your co-workers competent?
    Are they supportive?   Yes ☐   No ☐
    Are they competitive?   Yes ☐   No ☐
    Are co-workers mainly . . .   Male ☐   Female ☐
    If no, to any of the above, explain. _____

28. Is your supervisor competent?   Yes ☐   No ☐
    Is he/she supportive?   Yes ☐   No ☐
    Is he/she competitive?   Yes ☐   No ☐
    Is supervisor . . .   Male ☐   Female ☐
    Is no, to any of the above, explain. _____

29. Is there an active EEO.AA program in your firm?   Yes ☐   No ☐
    If yes, how has this program affected you and your job? Please explain.

30. How are you perceived by your co-workers? _____

31. Does this perception coincide with your own self-image? _____

32. Do you have responsibility and/or desire for "change" in the organization's policies and procedures? Please explain. _____
    If yes, how successful have you been with respect to designing/implementing these changes? _____

33. To what extent have you had to modify your own personal behavior/goals/ ideals in order to "fit" in the organization? Please explain.

34. How important is appearance (dress) on your job? _____

35. What type of dress is required for your work? _____

36. Are the physical conditions and layout of your office conducive to work?
            Yes ☐   No ☐

(Appendix B. continued overleaf)

Five-Year Follow-up Survey
Sloan School Class of

---

37. Do you have a mentor?   Yes ☐   No ☐
    If yes, (a) Who is/was your mentor? _____
            (b) Where does he/she fall in the organizational hierarchy? _____
            (c) How long has he/she served as your mentor? _____
            (d) Is/was there a significant difference in age between you and your
                mentor? _____
            (e) If you had a different mentor in the past, do you still maintain a
                mentor/mentee relationship with that person?   Yes ☐   No ☐
                i. Please specify where the former mentor is in the hierarchy
                   (currently) with respect to you. _____
                ii. How has the relationship changed? _____

38. (a) Is your mentor useful to you? _____
    (b) How does your mentor help you? _____

39. Have you served as mentor? Please explain. _____

40. (a) Have you experienced any problems related to stress in your worklife?
        Please explain the causes of this stress (i.e., role ambiguity, inadequacy
        in job, loss of discretionary responsibility, other).

    _____

    (b) How do you cope with this? _____

41. Has stress affected your performance at work?   Yes ☐   No ☐
    If yes, explain. _____

42. During the past five years have you left the workforce for any length of
    time?   Yes ☐   No ☐
    If yes, length _____ Reason: _____

        School ☐   Unemployed ☐
        Other   ☐

43. Have your career aspirations changed since the time you began work?
    Please explain. _____

44. Do you anticipate any job changes in the near future?   Yes ☐   No ☐
    If yes, explain. _____

45. Have you considered becoming an entrepreneur at some future time?

    _____

Five-Year Follow-up Survey
Sloan School Class of

---

46. Are you married (or the equivalent to you)?
    Yes ☐ Were you married prior to work, after Sloan School, or after start-
    ing work? _____
    No ☐ Do you plan to marry at some point in the future? Please explain.

---

47. (a) Do you have children?   Yes ☐   No ☐
        If no, do you plan to have children at some point in the future?
        Please explain. _____
    (b) If yes, ages: _____

48. What sort of child care arrangements do you have?

    Spouse at home ☐   Sitter at home ☐
    Day care ☐   School ☐
    Other ☐

49. Are the child care arrangements satisfactory?   Yes ☐   No ☐
    If no, why not? _____

50. How much time on the average do you spend with your child (children)
    during the work week? _____ hours/day; on days you do not work?
    _____ hours/day.

51. Are you in a dual-career relationship?   Yes ☐   No ☐ If yes,
    (a) How has your relationship affected your progress or performance at
        work (i.e., does it constrain, have no effect, facilitate, etc.). _____
    (b) Has your spouse progressed as far in his/her career as you have? What is
        spouse's occupation? _____
    (c) How has your career affected the relationship? _____
    (d) How has your spouse's career affected the relationship? _____

52. (a) How do household duties get done? (shopping, cleaning, cooking).
        Self ☐   Spouse ☐
        Other ☐
    (b) If more than one person is responsible, please give estimates of how
        work is divided (i.e., self 50%, spouse 50%). How many hours do you
        spend on these activities? _____

53. (a) How much do your job and personal life interfere with each other?
        A lot ☐   Somewhat ☐
        Not too much ☐   Not at all ☐
    (b) In what ways do they interfere? _____

(Appendix B. continued overleaf)

Five-Year Follow-up Survey
Sloan School Class of

---

54. Have you experienced any significant change in your personal life?
    Yes ☐   No ☐ If yes, explain. _____

    Marital Status   ☐   Children   ☐
    Health   ☐   Relocation   ☐
    Other   ☐

55. (a) How frequently do you participate in non-work related activities out-
        side the home? (i.e., concerts, sports events, movies etc.)
        Hours/month _____

    (b) Are you satisfied with this balance between work and non-work related
        activities?   Yes ☐   No ☐
        If no, how would you change this? _____

56. (a) Has stress affected your personal life? Please explain.

        _____

    (b) How do you cope with this? _____

57. Who do you feel provides you with the most support when problems arise at
    home or work?
        Spouse   ☐   Friend   ☐
        Peers at work   ☐   Mentor   ☐
        Other   ☐ (please indicate) _____

58. FOR ENTREPRENEURS:
    (a) When did you decide to change from the corporate or management
        consulting mode to entrepreneurship? _____

    (b) What were the primary reasons for the change? _____

    (c) Do you find it as satisfying as your non-entrepreneurial job?
        Yes ☐   No ☐ If no, why not? _____

    (d) Do you plan to spend the rest of your career as an entrepreneur? _____

    (e) Do you have a partner and does that person have skills that are
        complementary or supplementary to yours? _____

    (f) Do you think the Sloan School should have some courses designed for
        those who wish to be entrepreneurs? _____

    (g) If the business is family owned, do you expect to run it one day? _____

59. Five years from now, when you will have been away from the Sloan School
    for ten years, where do you expect to be in your career? _____

60. Currently, the Sloan School is reviewing its curriculum. Any comments or
    suggestions that you have are welcome.

Five-Year Follow-up Survey
Sloan School Class of

Additional Comments:

APPENDIX C

Private Sector Employers of Sloan Graduates[a]

Abbot Products, Inc.
Acushnet Company
Adams, Harkeness and Hill, Inc.
Advanced Information Systems and
  Services
Advanced Micro Devices, Inc.
Advantage Systems, Inc.
Air Power, Inc.
Air Products and Chemicals, Inc.
Alexander Grant and Company
Allendale Mutual Insurance
Alliance Tool Corporation
Allied Chemical
Alpha Industries, Inc.
Amdahl Corporation
American Airlines, Inc.
American Bell, Inc.
American Biltrite, Inc.
American Broadcasting Company
  (ABC)
American Can Company
American Cyanamid Company
American Edwards Laboratories
American Express Company
American Hospital Supply
  Corporation
American International Group, Inc.
American Management Systems, Inc.
American Optical Corporation
AMF
Amherst Associates
Analog Devices, Inc.
Analysts, (management & planning)
Arthur Andersen and Company
Anheuser-Busch
Apollo Computer, Inc.
Apple Computer, Inc.
ARAMCO
ARCO (Atlantic Richfield Oil Co.)
Armco Steel
Arthur Young and Company
Arvida Corporation
ATEX, Inc.
Bain and Company

Bank of America
Bankers Trust Company
Barber Blue Sea Lines
Barr Rosenberg Associates
Theodore Barry and Associates
Marshall Bartlett
Baxter Travenol Laboratories, Inc.
Bell Laboratories
Bendix Corporation
Sanford C. Bernstein
Black and Decker Manufacturing
  Company
Blue Cross/Blue Shield
Boeing Company
Boise Cascade Corporation
Bolt, Beranek, and Newman
Booz, Allen, and Hamilton, Inc.
Boston Consulting Group
Braxton Associates, Inc.
Burns, Jackson, Mellon, Summit,
  & Jacoby
Cambridge Research Associates
Cambridge Royalty Company
Carborundum Company
Charles River Associates
Charrette Corporation
Chase Manhattan Bank
Chicago Board Options Exchange
Children's Hospital
CIGNA Corporation
Citibank/Citicorp
Citizen and Southern National Bank
  of South Carolina
Columbia Broadcasting Systems (CBS)
Commercial Union Insurance
  Company
Comucard International
Compugraphic Corporation
Compumotor
Compuserve, Inc.
Computek
Computer Controls Corporation
Computer Corporation of America
  (Compucorp)

Connecticut General Life Insurance Company
Continental Bank of Illinois
Continental Group
Continental Oil Company
Coopers and Lybrand
Corning Glass Works
Courier Corporation
CRC Education and Human Development
Cresap, McCormick, Paget, Inc.
Crocker National Bank
Cybernetics
Data General Corporation
Data Resources, Inc.
Dean Witter Reynolds Company, Inc.
Decision Sciences Corporation
Deloitte, Haskins, and Sells
Diano Corporation
Digital Equipment Corporation (DEC)
Digital Research
Dillion Read
Donnelly Mirrors
Doubleday and Company
Drano Corporation
Dynamics Associates, Inc.
Dunnam Company
Eberstadt and Company, Inc.
E. F. Hutton
Elector Scientific Industry
EIL Corporation
Endowment Management and Research
Engelhard Corporation
Equitable Life Assurance Society
Execucom Systems Corporation
Exxon Chemical
Exxon International
Exxon Co., USA
Exxon Enterprises, Inc.
Exxon Research & Engineering Company
Fairfax Hospital Association
Federal Express Corporation
Federal Reserve Bank of Boston
Federal Reserve Bank of New York
Federal Reserve Board of Governors
First Boston Corporation
First Capital Companies
First Data Corporation
First National Bank of Boston
First National Bank of Chicago
Flying Tiger
FMC Corporation
Forbes Magazine
The Ford Motor Company
Fortune Magazine
Foster-Miller Association
Frito Lay
Garden Way, Inc.
General Electric Company
General Electric Credit Corporation
General Foods Corporation
General Motors Corporation
General Telephone and Electronics (GTE)
Genimar
Georgetown Consulting Group
Golden West Financial Corporation
Goldman, Sachs, and Company
Greenpoint Terminal Warehouse
Grops Valley Group
Gulf Oil Corporation
Hagler, Bailly, and Company
Hague Company, Inc. W. M.
Halifax Engineering
Harborside Corporation
Harbridge House, Inc.
Harris Corporation
Harris Trust Company
Hay Associaties
Health Systems, Inc.
Hertz Corporation
Hewlett-Packard Company
Home Box Office (HBO)
Hooker Chemical and Plastics Corporation
Hughes Aircraft
(E. F.) Hutton and Group, Inc.
International Business Machines (IBM)

(Appendix C. continued overleaf)

ICF, Inc.
Index Systems, Inc.
Indian Ridge Company
Inexco Oil Company
Information Strategies, Inc.
Intech Corporation
Integrated Technologies, Inc.
Intel Corporation
Interactive Data Corporation
International Finance Corporation
International Harvester Company
International Paper Company
Investors in Industry
Iomega Corporation
ITT Corporation
Jet Propulsion Laboratory
Johnson and Johnson
Kennecott Corporation
Killingsworth Liddy and Company
Land Resources Corporation
Lehman Brothers
Libbey-Owens Ford Company
Le Croy Research Systems
  Corporation
Arthur D. Little, Inc.
Lotus Development Corporation
Charles T. Main, Inc.
J. Makwoski Associates, Inc.
Management Analysis Center, Inc.
Management Decision Systems
Marshall Bartlett, Inc.
Martin Marietta Corporation
Mass. Financial Services, Inc.
MCI Telecommunications
McKinsey and Company, Inc.
Mead Corporation
Measurex Corporation
Mellon Bank, N.A.
Mellon National Mortgage Corporation
Merck and Company, Inc.
Meredith Associates, Inc.
Merrill Lynch and Company
Metpath, Inc.
Metromedia, Inc.
Microwave Associates
Minnesota Mining and Manufacturing
  Company

Mobil Oil Corporation
Morgan Guaranty Trust Company
Morgan Stanley and Company, Inc.
McCleod, Young, Weir Limited
McCraffery, Seligman and Von Simson
National Broadcasting Company, Inc.
  (NBC)
National Semi-Conductor Corporation
Nestlé Company, Inc.
Nippon Tel and Tel Public
  Corporation
North Shore Supply Company
Norton Company
Northville Industries
John Nuveen and Company
Occidental Chemical Holding
  Corporation
Omega
Paccar, Inc.
Peat, Marwick, Mitchell and Company
Pennzoil Company
Pepsico, Inc.
Perini Corporation
Polaroid Corporation
Polychrome Corporation
PPG Industries, Inc.
Precision Lithograining Corporation
Price, Waterhouse and Company
Prime Computer, Inc.
Prudential Insurance Company of
  America
The Procter and Gamble Company
Prudential-Bache Securities
Pugh-Roberts Associates, Inc.
Putnam, Hayes and Bartlett, Inc.
The Quaker Oats Company
Raychem Corporation
RCA Corporation
Reid Tool
Resource Planning Associates
R. J. Reynolds Industries, Inc.
John Rivera
Rolm Corporation
Ropes and Gray
Rush-Presbyterian/St. Luke Medical
  Center
Ryder System, Inc.

Saint Luke's Medical Center
Saddlebrook Corporation
Kurt Salmon Associates
Salomon Brothers, Inc.
Sandburn Waxworks, Inc.
Satellite Business Systems
Schlumberger Ltd.
Schreiber Cheese (L.D.)
Scribe Data Systems
G. D. Searle and Company
Shycon Associates
Siemens Corporation
Smart Software Development Firm
Smith, Kline, and French Corporation
Software Arts
Sonesta International Hotels
   Corporation
Southeast Banking Corporation
Southern Pacific Transportation
   Company
Standard Brands
Standard Oil of Indiana
State Street Bank and Trust Company
State Street Research and Management
   Company
Steiner Corporation
The Stop and Shop Companies
Strategic Planning Associates
Sun Company, Inc.
Technical Assistance and Training
   Corporation
Technomic Consultants

Tektronix, Inc.
Temple, Barker, and Sloane, Inc.
Texas Instruments, Inc.
Tiger International, Inc.
TMI Systems Corporation
Touche Ross and Company
Towers, Perrin, Forster and Crosby
TRW, Inc.
TRW Communications System
TWA
Twain Associates
Tymshare Corporation
UDD
Union Carbide Corporation
United Brands
Unitrode Corporation
U.S. Lines
U.S. Scientific Instrument Company
Vitalink Communications
Wang Laboratories, Inc.
Wasserman and Associates, Inc.
Wells Fargo Bank, N.A.
Westinghouse (Group W/Cable)
Westinghouse Defense Electronics
Westvaco Corporation
Weyerhaeuser Company
Wheelabrator Frye
Whittaker Corporation
Willow Company
World Bank
Xerox Corporation
Zayre

---

a. Does not include self-employed, family enterprises, and consulting organizations of less than five persons.

BIBLIOGRAPHY

GENERAL

Argyris, Chris. *Personality and Organization.* New York: Harper & Row, 1957.

Arthur, M.B., L. Bailyn, D. Levinson, H. Shepard. *Working With Careers.* New York: Center for Research in Career Development, Graduate School of Business, Columbia University, 1984.

Berton, Lee. "Touche Ross and Co. Buys Braxton, Inc." *The Wall Street Journal*, December 4, 1984.

Ghiselli, Edwin E. *Explorations In Managerial Talent.* Pacific Palisades, Calif.: Goodyear Publishing Co., Inc. 1971.

Hale, Henry C., and Patel, Homi K. "Female First Line Supervisors: Prescriptions, Problems, and Performance." Master's thesis, Sloan School of Management, Massachusetts Institute of Technology, 1979.

Herzberg, Frederick. *Work: On the Nature of Man.* New York: World Publishers, 1966.

Hunt, David M., and Carol, Michael. "Mentorship: A Career Training and Development Tool." *Academy of Management Review* 8 (1983): 475-85.

Ivancevich, John, and Michael Matteson. *Stress and Work: A Managerial Perspective.* Glenview, Ill.: Scott, Foresman and Co., 1980.

Kam, C.W. "Upward Mobility of Young Managers: A Study of Management Information System Personnel." Master's thesis, Sloan School of Management, Massachusetts Institute of Technology, 1985.

Keen, Peter. "Cognitive Style and Career Specialization." In J. Van Maanen, ed., *Organizational Careers: Some New Perspectives*, ch. 4, pp. 89-105. New York: John Wiley and Sons, 1977.

Koontz, Harold. "The Management Theory Jungle Re-Visited." *Academy of Management Review* 5 (April 1980): 175–87.

Kotter, John P. *The General Managers.* New York: The Free Press, 1982.

Kotter, John P. *Power and Influence.* New York: The Free Press, 1985.

Levine, Chester. "Miscellaneous Business Services: Little Known But Growing Fast." *Occupational Outlook Quarterly* 29 (Summer 1985): 20–25.

Maccoby, M. *The Gamesman: The New Corporate Leaders.* New York: Simon and Schuster, 1976.

Malone, Thomas W.; Joanne Yates; and Robert I. Benjamin. "Electronic Markets and Electronic Hierarchies." *Communications of the Association for Computing Machinery* 30 (June 1987): 484–97.

Maslow, Abraham. "A Theory of Human Motivation." *Psychological Review* 50 (1943): 370–96.

McClelland, David. "Toward A Theory of Motive Acquisitions." *American Psychologist* 20 (1965): 321–33.

McGregor, Douglas. *The Human Side of Enterprise.* New York: McGraw-Hill Book Co., 1960.

Mintzberg, Henry. *The Nature of Managerial Work.* New York: Harper & Row, 1973.

Mitchell, Terrence. "Expectancy Models of Job Satisfaction, Occupational Preference and Effort: A Theoretical Methodological and Empirical Appraisal." *Psychological Bulletin* 81 (1982): 1053–77.

National Center for Education Statistics. *Digest of Educational Statistics.* Washington, D.C.: U.S. Government Printing Office, various years.

Okun, Arthur M. *Prices and Quantities.* Washington, D.C.: The Brookings Institution, 1981.

Osterman, Paul. *Employment Futures: Reorganization, Dislocation, and Public Policy.* Vol. 2. New York: Oxford University Press, 1988.

Pfeffer, Jeffrey. "Effects of an MBA and Socio-Economic Origins in Business School Graduates' Salaries." *Journal of Applied Psychology* 62 (1977): 698–703.

Roche, Gerard E. "Much Ado About Mentors." *Harvard Business Review* 57 (1979): 17–28.

Rockart, J.F., and M.S. Scott Morton. "Implications of Changes in Information Technology for Corporation Strategy." *Interfaces* 14 (January/February 1984): 84–95.

Rosenbaum, James E. *Career Mobility in A Corporate Hierarchy.* Orlando, Fla.: Academic Press, 1984.

Schein, Edgar H. *Career Dynamics: Matching Individual and Organizational Needs.* Reading, Mass.: Addison-Wesley Publishing Co., 1978.

Tenenbaum, Elizabeth B. "The Post-Doctoral MBA: A Study in Career Change." Master's thesis, Sloan School of Management, Massachusetts Institute of Technology, 1982.

Tilney, Cathleen. "Stress and MBA's." Master's thesis, Sloan School of Management, Massachusetts Institute of Technology, 1982.

U.S. Bureau of the Census. *Earnings in 1983 of Married-Couple Families, By Characteristics of Husbands and Wives.* Series p-60 No. 153. Washington, D.C.: U.S. Government Printing Office, 1986.

U.S. Bureau of the Census. *Money, Income and Poverty Status of Families and Persons in the United States.* Series P 60, No. 149. Washington, D.C.: U.S. Government Printing Office, 1985.

U.S. Office of Management and Budget. *Standard Industrial Classification Manual.* Washington, D.C.: U.S. Government Printing Office, 1972.

Van Mannen, John, ed. *Organizational Careers: Some New Perspectives.* New York: John Wiley and Sons, 1977.

Veiga, John F. "Mobility Influences During Managerial Career Stages." *Academy of Management Journal* 26 (March 1983): 64–85.

Weinstein, Alan G., and V. Srimivasan. "Predicting Managerial of Master of Business Administration (MBA) Graduates." *Journal of Applied Psychology* 59, no. 2 (1974): 207–12.

Wren, Daniel. *The Evolution of Management Thought.* Third edition. New York: John Wiley and Sons, 1987.

Yankelovitch, Daniel. *The New Rules.* New York: Randon House, 1981.

Zuboff, Shoshana. *In the Age of the Smart Machine.* New York: Basic Books, 1988.

WOMEN MANAGERS

Abramson, J. *Old Boys, New Women: The Politics of Sex Discrimination.* New York: Praeger Publishers, 1979.

Adams, J. *Women at the Top.* New York: Hawthorn Books, 1979.

"Advancement for Women in Hierarchial Organizations: A Multilevel Analysis of Problems and Solutions." *Journal of Applied Behavioral Science* 19 (1983): 19-33.

Allen, F. "Women Managers Get Paid Far Less Than Males Despite Career Gains." *The Wall Street Journal*, October 7, 1980.

Almquist, E. M. *Minorities, Gender and Work.* Lexington, Mass.: Lexington Books, 1979.

Almquist, E. M., and S. C. Angrist. "Career Salience and Typicality of Occupational Choice Among College Women." *Journal of Marriage and the Family* 32 (May 1970): 242-49.

Amsden, A., ed. *The Economics of Women and Work.* New York: St. Martin's Press, 1980.

Badawy, M. K. "How Women Managers View Their Role in the Organization." *The Personnel Administrator* 23 (February 1978): 60-68.

Bailyn, L. "Accommodation of Work to Family." In R. Rapoport and R. N. Rapoport, eds., *Working Couples*, ch. 12, pp. 159-74. New York: Harper & Row, Publishers, Inc., 1973

Bailyn, L. "The Apprenticeship Model of Organizational Careers." In P. A. Wallace, ed., *Women in the Workplace*, ch. 3, pp. 45–58. Boston, Mass.: Auburn House Publishing Co., 1982.

Bailyn, L. "The 'Slow Burn' Way to the Top: Some Thoughts on the Early Years of Organizational Careers." In C. B. Derr, ed., *Work, Family, and the Career: New Frontiers in Theory and Research*, ch. 6, pp. 94–105. New York: Praeger Publishers, 1980.

Bartol, K. M., and D. A. Butterfield. "Sex Effects in Evaluating Leaders." *Journal of Applied Psychology* 61 (August 1976): 446–54.

Bartol, K. M., and P. J. Manhardt. "Sex Differences in Job Outcome Preferences: Trends Among New Hired College Graduates." *Journal of Applied Psychology* 64 (October 1979): 447–82.

Basil, D. C. *Women in Management*. New York: Dunellen Books, 1972.

Baum, L. "Corporate Women: They're About to Break Through to the Top." *Business Week*, June 22, 1987.

Beckhard, R. "Managerial Careers in Transition: Dilemmas and Directions." In J. Van Mannen, ed., *Organizational Careers: Some New Perspectives*, ch. 7 pp. 149–60. New York: John Wiley and Sons, 1977.

Beller, A. "Occupational Segregation by Sex and Race, 1960–1981." In B. Reskin, ed., *Sex Segregation in the Workplace*, ch. 2, pp. 11–26. Washington, D.C.: National Academy Press, 1984.

Bergmann, B. R. *The Economic Emergence of Women*. New York: Basic Books, 1986.

Berlew, D. E., and D. T. Hall. "The Socialization of Managers: Effects of Expectations on Performance." *Administrative Science Quarterly* 1 (September 1966): 207–23.

Biogness, W. J. "Effect of Applicant's Sex, Race, and Employers' Performance Ratings: Some Additional Findings." *Journal of Applied Psychology* 61 (February 1976): 80–84.

Birdsall, P. "A Comparative Analysis of Male and Female Managerial Communications Styles in Two Organizations." *Journal of Vocational Behavior* 16 (April 1980): 183–96.

Blau, F. D., and M. A. Ferber. *The Economic of Women, Men and Work*. Englewood Cliffs, N.J.: Prentice-Hall, 1986.

Blau, F. D., and M. A. Ferber. "Occupations and Earnings of Women Workers." In K. S. Koziara; M. H. Moskow; and L. D. Tanner, eds., *Working Women: Past, Present, Future*, ch. 2, pp. 37–68. Washington, D.C.: The Bureau of National Affairs, 1987.

"Boosting the Careers of B-School Grads." *Business Week*, October 11, 1982.

Bowman, G.; N. B. Worthy; and S. A. Greyser. "Are Women Executives People?" *Harvard Business Review* 43 (July–August 1965): 14–28, 164–78.

Braun, H., III. "MBA Salaries: Do Women Earn as Much as Men?" Master's thesis, Sloan School of Management, Massachusetts Institute of Technology, 1985.

Bray, D. W. "The Assessment Center: Opportunities for Women." *Personnel* 48 (September-October 1971): 30–34.

Bray, D. W.; R. J. Campbell; and D. L. Grant. *Formative Years in Business: A Long-Term AT&T Study of Managerial Lives.* New York: John Wiley and Sons, 1974.

"Breaking Through to the Top." *Working Women* (April 1985): 97–119.

Brown, L. K. "Women and Business Management." *Signs* 5 (1979): 266–88.

Brown, L. K. "Women in Business Management." In *Notes: Program in Sex Roles and Social Change.* New York: Center for Social Sciences, Columbia University, 1980.

Buono, A. F., and J. B. Kamm. "Marginality and the Organizational Socialization of Female Managers." *Human Relations* 36 (1983): 1125–40.

Campbell, J. P.; M. D. Dunnette; E. E. Lawler, III; and K. E. Weick, Jr. *Managerial Behavior, Performance and Effectiveness.* New York: McGraw-Hill Book Co., 1970.

Cherpas, C. C. "Dual-Career Families: Terminology, Typologies, and Work and Family Issues." *Journal of Counseling and Development* 63 (June 1985): 616–20.

Clawson, J. G. "Mentoring in Managerial Careers." In C. B. Derr, ed., *Work, Family, and the Career: New Frontiers in Theory and Research*, ch. 8, pp. 144–65. New York: Praeger Publishers, 1980.

Clawson, J. G. *On Mentors, Developmental Relationships and Women in Management.* Working Paper HBS 80–54. Boston, Mass.: Graduate School of Business Administration, Harvard University, 1980.

Collins, G. "Unforseen Business Barriers for Women." *The New York Times*, May 31, 1982.

Cook, S. H., and J. L. Mendelson. "The Power Wielders: Men and Women Managers?" *Industrial Management* 26 (March-April 1984): 22–27.

Cooper, C. L., and M. J. Davidson. "The High Cost of Stress on Women Managers." *Organizational Dynamics* 10 (Spring 1982): 44–53.

"The Corporate Woman: Up The Ladder—Finally." *Business Week*, November 2, 1975.

"Corporations and Two-Career Families: Directions for the Future." *Catalyst*, 1981.

Cottle, T. J. "Contrasting Men's and Women's Perceptions of Time." In T. J. Cottle, ed., *Perceiving Time*, pp. 80–81. New York: John Wiley and Sons, 1976.

Cottle, T. J., ed. *Perceiving Time*, ch. 11, pp. 169–94. New York: John Wiley and Sons, 1976.

Crittenden, V. L., and W. F. Crittenden. "Male and Female Students' Perceptions of Women in Management." *Collegiate News and Views* 36 (Spring 1983): 27–31.

Crocker, J., ed. "After Affirmative Actions: Barriers to Occupational Advancement for Women and Minorities." *American Behavioral Scientist* 27 (January/February 1984): 283–407.

Davidson, M., and C. Cooper. *Stress and the Woman Manager.* New York: St. Martin's Press, 1983.

Deaux, K. "From Individual Differences to Social Categories: Analysis of a Decade's Research on Gender." *American Psychologist* 39 (February 1984): 105–16.

Derr, B. C., ed. *Work, Family, and the Career.* New York: Praeger Publishers, 1980.

Devanna, M. A. "Male/Female Careers, The First Decade." New York: Center for Research in Career Development, Graduate School of Business, Columbia University, 1984.

Dipboye, R. L. "Problems and Progress of Women in Management." In K. S. Koziara; M. H. Moskow; and L. D. Tanner, eds. *Working Women*, ch. 5, pp. 118–53. Washington, D.C.: The Bureau of National Affairs, Inc., 1987.

Donnell, S., and J. Hall. "Men and Women as Managers: A Significant Case of No Significant Differences." *Organizational Dynamics* 8 (Spring 1980): 60–77.

Doudna, C. "Women at the Top." *New York Times Magazine* (November 30, 1980): 54–55, 115–20.

Drazin, R., and E. R. Auster. "Wage Differences Between Men and Women: Performance Appraisal Ratings vs. Salary Allocation as the Locus of Bias." *Human Resource Management* 26 (Summer 1987): 157–68.

Dubno, P. "Attitudes Toward Women Executives: A Longitudinal Approach." *Academy of Management Journal* 28 (1985): 235–39.

Epstein, C. E. "Encountering the Male Establishment: Sex-Status Limits on Women's Careers in the Professions." *American Journal of Sociology* 75 (1970): 965–82.

Farley, J., ed. *The Women in Management.* Ithaca, N.Y.: ILR Press, New York State School of Industrial and Labor Relations, Cornell University, 1983.

Fernandez, J. P. *Racism and Sexism in Corporate Life.* Lexington, Mass.: Lexington Books, 1981.

Ferber, M. A., and B. Kordick. "Sex Differences in the Earnings of Ph. Ds." *Industrial and Labor Relations Review* 31 (January 1978): 227–38.

Fisher, A. B. "Where Women Are Succeeding." *Fortune* 116 (August 3, 1987): 78–86.

Fischl, P. W. "Mentoring and Developmental Relationships Between Senior Executive Women and Junior Female Managers." Master's thesis, Sloan School of Management, Massachusetts Institute of Technology, 1986.

Fitt, L. W., and D. A. Newton. "When the Mentor Is a Man and the Protege a Woman." *Harvard Business Review* 59 (March-April 1981): 56–60.

Forbes, J. B., and J. E. Piercy. "Rising to the Top: Executive Women in 1983 and Beyond." *Business Horizons* 26 (September-October 1983): 38–47.

Fowler, E. M. "Women as Senior Executives." *The New York Times*, November 10, 1982.

Fraker, S. "Why Women Aren't Getting to the Top." *Fortune* 109 (April 16, 1984): 40–45.

Frieze, I. H., and B. H. Hanusa. "Women Scientists: Overcoming Barriers." In M. Steinkamp, and M. Maehr, eds., *Women in Science: Advances in Motivation and Achievement*. Greenwood, Conn.: JAI Press, 1984.

Gallese, L. R. *Women Like Us.* New York: William Morrow and Co., Inc., 1985.

Gallese, L. R. "Family Doesn't Keep Women from Getting Ahead." *The Wall Street Journal*, May 4, 1981.

Garland, H., and K. H. Price. "Attitudes Toward Women in Management and Attributions for Their Success and Failure in a Managerial Position." *Journal of Applied Psychology* 62 (1977): 29–33.

Garland, H.; K. Hale; and M. Burnson. "Attributions for the Success and Failure of Female Managers: A Replication and Extensions." *Psychology of Women Quarterly* 7 (Winter 1982): 155–62.

Gilbert, L. A. *Men in Dual Career Families: Current Realities and Future Prospects.* Hillside, N. J.: Lawrence Erlbaum Associates, 1985.

Gilligan, C. *In a Different Voice.* Cambridge, Mass.: Harvard University Press, 1982.

Ginzberg, E., and A. M. Yohalem, eds. *Corporate Lib: Women's Challenge to Management.* Baltimore: Johns Hopkins University Press, 1973.

Gluckson, R. "Women MBAs in the Eighties: Stepping Off the Corporate Ladder." *Journal of College Placement* 45 (Summer 1985): 41–44.

Gordon, F. E., and M. H. Strober. "Initial Observations on a Pioneer Cohort: 1974 Women MBAs." *Sloan Management Review* 19 (Winter 1978): 15–23.

Gordon, F. E., and M. H. Strober. *Bringing Women into Management.* New York: McGraw-Hill Book Co., 1975.

Gordon, F. E., and D. T. Hall. "Self-Image and Sterotypes of Femininity: Their Relationship to Women's Role Conflicts and Coping." *Journal of Applied Psychology* 59 (1974): 241–3.

Gottschalk, E. C., Jr. "Distaff Owners: More Women Start Up Their Own Business, With Major Successes." *The Wall Street Journal*, May 17, 1983.

Grant, Jan. "Women as Managers: What They Can Offer to Organizations." *Organizational Dynamics* 16 (Winter 1988): 56–63.

Gross, J. "Against the Odds." *The New York Times Magazine*, January 6, 1985.

Gunderson, M. "The Influence of the Status and Sex Composition of Occupations on the Male-Female Earnings Gap." *Industrial and Labor Relations Review* 31 (January 1978): 217–26.

Gutek, B., and L. Larwood, eds. *Women's Career Development.* Newbury Park, Calif.: Sage Publications, 1987.

Hagen, R. L., and A. Kahn. "Discrimination Against Competent Women." *Journal of Applied Social Psychology* 5 (1975): 362–76.

Hale, R. W., and J. A. Drummond. "The Effect of the Dual-Career Marriage on Female Managers in Two Large Multi State Companies." Master's thesis, Sloan School of Management, Massachusetts Institute of Technology, 1979.

Hall, D. T. "A Model of Coping with Role Conflict: The Role Behavior of College Educated Women." *Administrative Science Quarterly* 17 (December 1972): 471-86.

Hall, D. T., and F. S. Hall. "Stress and the Two-Career Couple." In C. L. Cooper and R. Payne, eds., *Current Concerns in Occupational Stress*, ch. 9, pp. 243-68. John Wiley and Sons, 1980.

Hall, F. S., and D. T. Hall. *The Two Career Couple*. Reading, Mass.: Addison-Wesley Publishing Co., 1979.

Hall, F. S., and D. T. Hall. "Effects of Job Incumbents' Race and Sex on Evaluations of Managerial Performance." *Academy of Management Journal* 19 (September 1976): 476-81.

Hardesty, S., and J. Nehama. *Success and Betrayal: The Crisis of Women in Corporate America*. New York: Franklin Watts, 1986.

Harlan, A. "The Woman MBA." 1978. (Unpublished.)

Harlan, A. *A Comparison of Careers for Male and Female MBAs*. Wellesley, Mass.: Center for Research on Women. Wellesley College, 1978. (Unpublished.)

Harlan, A. *MBA Goals and Aspirations: Potential Predictors of Later Success Differences Between Males and Females*. Paper for the meeting of the National Academy of Management, August 1976.

Harlan, A., and C. L. Weiss. *Moving Up: Women in Managerial Careers: Final Report*. Wellesley, Mass.: Center for Research on Women, Wellesley College, 1981.

Harlan, A., and C. L. Weiss. "Sex Differences in Factors Affecting Managerial Career Advancement." In P. A. Wallace, ed., *Women in the Workplace*, ch. 4, pp. 59-100. Boston, Mass.: Auburn House Publishing Co., 1982.

Harrell, T., and M. Harrell. "Careers of Women, Minority and White Male MBAs." Research Paper No. 558. Stanford, Calif.: Graduate School of Business, Stanford University, 1981.

Harrell, T., and B. Alpert. "MBAs, Twenty Years After." Research Paper No. 750. Stanford, Calif.: Graduate School of Business, Stanford University, 1985.

Harriman, A. *Women/Men/Management*. New York: Praeger Publishers, 1985.

Hayghe, H. "Dual-Career Families: Their Economic and Demographic Characteristics." In J. Aldous, ed., *Two Paychecks: Life in Dual Earner Families*, ch. 2, pp. 27-40. Beverly Hills, Calif.: Sage Publications, 1982.

Heidrick and Struggles, Inc. *The Corporate Women Offices*. Chicago: Heidrick and Struggles, 1986.

Hennig, M., and A. Jardin. *The Managerial Woman*. New York: Anchor Press, 1977.

Herbert, T. T., and E. B. Yost. "Women as Effective Managers . . . A Strategic Model for Overcoming the Barriers." *Human Resource Management* 17 (Spring 1978): 18-25.

Hertz, R. *More Equal Than Others: Women and Men in Dual-Career Marriages.* Berkeley, Calif.: University of California Press, 1986.

Horner, M. "The Motive to Avoid Success and Changing Aspirations of College Women." In J. M. Bardwick, ed., *Readings on the Psychology of Women,* pp. 62-67. New York: Harper & Row, 1972.

Houston, L. "Business Womanly Wiles, A Few Rules on Disarming the Skeptics." *Master in Business Administration* (September 1977): 30-31.

Huck, J. R., and D. W. Bray. "Management Assessment Center Evaluations and Subsequent Job Performance of White and Black Females." *Personnel Psychology* 29 (Spring 1976): 13-30.

Hunt, J. G., and L. L. Hunt. "Dilemmas and Contradictions of Status: The Case of the Dual-Career Family." *Social Problems* 24 (1977): 407-16.

Hymowitz, C. "Male Workers and Female Bosses are Confronting Hard Challenge." *The Wall Street Journal,* July 16, 1984.

Hymowitz, C.; S. Rupert; and T. D. Schellhardt. "The Glass Ceiling: Why Women Can't Seem to Break the Invisible Barrier That Blocks Them from the Top Jobs." *The Wall Street Journal,* March 24, 1986.

Ilgen, D. R., and J. R. Terborg. "Sex Discrimination and Sex-Role Stereotypes: Are They Synonymous? No!" *Organizational Behavior and Human Performance* 14 (1975): 154-57.

Izraeli, D. N. "The Middle Manager and the Tactics of Power Expansion: A Case Study." *Sloan Management Review* 16 (Winter 1975): 57-70.

"Mrs. Jaffee Joins 53 Men in Citibank Senior Post." *The New York Times,* January 5, 1979.

Janes, M. J. "Career Anchors of Business and Professional Women." Master's thesis, Sloan School of Management, Massachusetts Institute of Technology, 1982.

Jelinek, M., and A. Harlan. *MBA Goals and Aspirations: Potential Predictors of Later Success Differences Between Males and Females.* Paper for the National Academy of Management, August, 1980.

Jenkins, R. L.; R. C. Reitzenstein; and F. G. Rodgers. "Report Cards on the MBA." *Harvard Business Review* (September-October 1984): 20-30.

Kanter, R. M. *The Change Masters: Innovations for Productivity in the American Corporation.* New York: Simon and Schuster, 1983.

Kanter, R. M. "Women Managers: Moving Up in a High Tech Society." In J. Farley, ed., *The Woman in Management,* ch. 3, pp. 21-33. Ithaca, N. Y.: Industrial and Labor Relations Press, 1983.

Kanter, R. M. "The Impact of Hierarchical Structures on the Work Behavior of Women and Men." In R. Kahn-Hut et al., *Women and Work,* ch. 16, pp. 234-47. New York: Oxford University Press, 1982.

Kanter, R. M. *Men and Women of the Corporation.* New York: Basic Books, 1977.

Korn/Ferry International. *Profile of Women Senior Executives.* Los Angeles, Calif.: Korn/Ferry International, 1982.

Kotter, J. P. *Power and Influence.* New York: The Free Press, 1985.

Koziara, K. S.; M. H. Moskow; and L. D. Tanner. *Working Women: Past, Present, Future.* Washington, D.C.: The Bureau of National Affairs, 1987.

Kram, K. E. *Mentoring at Work.* Glenview, Ill.: Scott, Foresman and Co., 1985.

Kryger, B. R., and R. Shikiar. "Sexual Discrimination in the Use of Letters of Recommendation: A Case of Reverse Discrimination." *Journal of Applied Psychology* 63 (1978): 309–14.

Larwood, C., and M. M. Wood. *Women in Management.* Lexington, Mass.: Lexington Books, 1977.

Larwood, L.; A. H. Stromberg; and B. A. Gutek, eds. *Women and Work.* Beverly Hills, Calif.: Sage Publications, 1985.

Lee, M. D., and B. L. Toffler. *Educational Career, and Personal Life Choices of Male and Female Managers.* Working Paper No. 81–94. Graduate School of Business Administration, Harvard University, 1981.

Lindholm, J. *Mentoring: The Mentor's Perspective.* Ph.D. dissertation, Sloan School of Management, Massachusetts Institute of Technology, 1984.

Loring, R., and T. Wells. *Breakthrough: Women into Management.* New York: Van Nostrand Reinhold Co., 1972.

"Losing the Salary Game." *The New York Times,* February 20, 1983.

Maccoby, E. E., and C. N. Jacklin. *The Psychology of Sex Differences.* Stanford, Calif.: Stanford University Press, 1974.

Madden, J. F. "The Persistence of Pay Differentials." In L. Larwood; A. H. Stromberg; and B. A. Gutek, eds., *Women and Work,* ch. 3, pp. 76–114. Beverly Hills, Calif.: Sage Publications, 1985.

Major, B., and E. Konar. "An Investigation of Sex Difference in Pay Expectations and Their Possible Causes." *Academy of Management Journal* 27 (December 1984): 777–92.

Mannheimer, T. S. "The Dual-Career Family: A Critical Analysis." Master's thesis, Sloan School of Management, Massachusetts Institute of Technology, 1976.

Marini, M. M., and E. Greenberger. "Sex Differences in Occupational Aspirations and Expectations." *Sociology of Work and Occupations* 5 (May 1978): 147–78.

Marshall, J. *Women Managers: Travellers in a Male World.* New York: John Wiley and Sons, 1984.

Mason, K. O.; J. L. Czajka; and S. Arber. "Change in U.S. Women's Sex-Role Attitudes, 1964–1974." *American Sociological Review* 41 (August 1976): 573–96.

Masengill, D., and N. Di Mario. "Sex Role Stereotypes and Requisite Management Characteristics: A Current Replication." *Sex-Roles* 5 (October 1979): 561–70.

Matteson, M. T. "Attitudes Toward Women as Managers: Sex or Role Differences?" *Psychological Reports* 39 (1976): 66.

McLane, H. J. *Selecting, Developing, and Retaining Women Executives.* New York: Van Nostrand Reinhold Co., 1980.

Megaree, E. I. "Influence of Sex Roles on the Manifestation of Leadership." *Journal of Applied Psychology* 53 (1979): 377–82.

Miner, J. B. "Motivation to Manage Among Women: Studies of Business Managers and Educational Administration." *Journal of Vocational Behavior* 5 (1974): 197–208.

Missirian, A. K. "The Female Manager as a Shelf-Sitter." *Human Resource Management* 17 (Winter 1978): 29–32.

Missirian, A. K. *The Corporate Connection: Why Executive Women Need Mentors to Reach the Top.* Englewood Cliffs, N. J.: Prentice-Hall, 1982.

Moore, L. L., ed. *Not As Far As You Think.* Lexington, Mass.: Lexington Books, 1986.

Moore, L. M., and A. V. Rickel. "Characteristics of Women in Traditional and Non-Traditional Managerial Roles." *Personnel Psychology* 33 (Summer 1980): 317–33.

Moses, J. L., and V. R. Boehm. "Relationship of Assessment-Center Performance to Management Progress of Women." *Journal of Applied Psychology* 54 (1975): 527–29.

Nemy, E. "The Top Women in Business Join Forces." *The New York Times,* March 7, 1983.

Notman, M. T.; C. C. Nadelson; and M. B. Bennett. "Achievement Conflict in Women." The Psychotherapeutic Process Proceedings, 10th International Congress of Psychotherapy, Paris in *Psychotherapy and Psychosomatics* 29 (1976): 203–13.

Olson, C. A., and B. E. Becker. "Sex Discrimination in the Promotion Process." *Industrial and Labor Relations Review* 36 (July 1983): 624–41.

Olson, J. E.; I. H. Frieze; and D. Good. "The Effects of Job Types and Industry on The Income of Male and Female MBA's." *The Journal of Human Resources* 22 (Fall 1987): 532–41.

Olson, J. E., and I. Hanson. "The Impact of Marriage, Children and Husband's Income on the Income of a Group of Highly Educated Women." Paper for the Eastern Economics Association Meeting, Pittsburgh, Pennsylvania, March 21–23, 1985.

"The 100 Top Corporate Women." *Business Week* (June 21, 1976): 56–68.

Pepitone-Rockwell, F., ed. *Dual-Career Couples.* Beverly Hills, Calif.: Sage Publications, 1980.

Petty, M. M., and R. H. Miles. "Leader Sex-Role Stereotyping in a Female-Dominated Work Culture." *Personnel Psychology* 29 (Autumn 1976): 393–404.

Pfeffer, J., and J. Ross. "The Effects of Marriage and a Working Wife on Occupational and Wage Attainment." *Administrative Science Quarterly* 27 (March 1982): 66–80.

Pfeifer, P., and S. J. Shapiro. "Male and Female MBA Candidates: Are There Personality Differences?" *Business Quarterly* 43 (Spring 1978): 77–80.

Phillips, L. L. *Mentors and Proteges: A Study of the Career Development of Women Managers and Executives in Business and Industry.* Ph.D. dissertation, University of California (Los Angeles), 1977.

Pleck, J. H., and G. L. Staines. "Work Schedules and Work-Family Conflicts in Two-Earner Couples." In J. Aldous, ed., *Two Paychecks: Life and Dual Earner Families.* Beverly Hills, Calif.: Sage Publications, 1982, ch. 4, pp. 63–87.

"Productivity of Working Women: Patterns, Problems, Solutions." *Catalyst,* New York: Women Directors' Roundtable, 1981.

Rapoport, R., and R. N. Rapoport. "The Next Generation in Dual-Earner Family Research." In J. Aldous, ed., *Two Paychecks: Life in Dual Earner Families,* ch. 12, pp. 229–43. Beverly Hills, Calif.: Sage Publications, 1982.

Rapoport, R., and R. N. Rapoport. "Three Generations of Dual Career Family Research." In F. Pepitone-Rockwell, *Dual Career Couples,* ch. 1, pp. 23–48. Beverly Hills, Calif.: Sage Publications, 1980.

Reder, M. "An Analysis of a Small, Closely Observed Labor Market: Starting Salaries for the University of Chicago M.B.A.s." *Journal of Business* 5 (April 1978): 263–97.

Reif, W. E.; J. W. Newstrom; and R. St. Louis, Jr. "Sex as a Discriminating Variable in Organizational Reward Decisions." *Academy of Management Journal* 19 (September 1976): 469–76.

Reitman, F. "MBA Career Paths—Are They Different For Men and Women?" Paper for the Academy of Management Meeting, San Diego, California, August 12, 1985.

Rice, D. G. *Dual Career Marriage: Conflict and Treatment.* New York: The Free Press, 1979.

Robertson, W. "Women MBAs, Harvard '73—How They're Doing." *Fortune* 98 (August 28, 1978): 50–60.

Robertson, W. "The Ten Highest-Ranking Women in Big Business." *Fortune* 87 (April 1973): 80–89.

Robinowitz, C. B.; C. C. Nadelson; and M. T. Notman. "Women in Academic Psychiatry: Politics and Progress." *American Journal of Psychiatry* 138 (October 1981): 1347–61.

Rogan, H. "Executive Women Find it Difficult to Balance Demands of Job, Home." *The Wall Street Journal,* October 30, 1984.

Rogan, H. "Top Women Executives Find Path to Power is Strewn With Hurdles." *The Wall Street Journal*, October 25, 1984.

Rogan, H. "Women Executives Feel That Men Both Aid and Hinder Their Careers." *The Wall Street Journal*, October 29, 1984.

Rogan, H. "Young Executive Women Advance Further, Faster Than Predecessors." *The Wall Street Journal*, October 26, 1984.

Rosen, B., and T. H. Jerdee. "Sex Stereotyping in the Executive Suite." *Harvard Business Review* 52 (March-April 1974): 45–58.

Rosen, B., and T. H. Jerdee. "Influence of Sex Role Stereotypes on Personnel Decisions." *Journal of Applied Psychology* 59 (1974): 9–14.

Rosen, B.; M. E. Templeton; and K. Kichline. "The First Few Years On the Job: Women in Management." *Business Horizons* 24 (November/December 1981): 26–29.

Rosenbaum, J. E. "Organizational Career Mobility: Promotion Chances in a Corporation During Periods of Growth and Contraction." *American Journal of Sociology* 85 (July 1979): 21–48.

Rowan, R. "How Harvard's Women MBAs Are Managing." *Fortune* 108 (July 11, 1983): 57–64.

Rowe, M. P. "Case of the Valuable Vendors." *Harvard Business Review* 56 (September-October, 1978): 40–60.

Reskin, B. F., ed. *Sex Segregation in the Workplace*. Washington, D.C.: National Academy Press, 1984.

Schanberg, S. H. "Keeping Women Out." *The New York Times*, September 18, 1984.

Schein, V. E. "Relationships Between Sex Role Stereotypes and Requisite Management Characteristics Among Female Managers." *Journal of Applied Psychology* 60 (1975): 340–44.

Schein, V. E. "The Women Industrial Psychologist: Illusion or Reality?" *American Psychologist* 26 (August 1971): 708–12.

Schneier, C. R. "The Contingency Model of Leadership: An Extension to the Emergent Leadership and Leader's Sex." *Organizational Behavior and Human Performance* 21 (April 1978): 220–39.

Schreiber, C. T. "Changing Places: Men and Women in Transitional Occupations." Cambridge, Mass.: MIT Press, 1979.

Schwartz, E. G. *The Sex Barrier in Business*. Atlanta, Ga.: Georgia State University Press, 1971.

Sekaran, U. "How Husbands and Wives in Dual-Career Families Perceive Their Family and Work Worlds." *Journal of Vocational Behavior* 22 (June 1983): 288–302.

Shaeffer, R. G., and E. F. Lynton. "Corporate Experiences in Improving Women's Job Opportunities." New York: The Conference Board, 1979.

Smith, R. E., ed. *The Subtle Revolution*. Washington, D.C.: The Urban Institute, 1979.

Stead, B. A. *Women in Management*. 2nd ed. Englewood Cliffs, N.J. Prentice-Hall, Inc. 1985.

Stein, B. *Getting There: Patterns in Managerial Success*. Working Paper. Wellesley, Mass.: Center for Research on Women, Wellesley College, 1976.

Steinberg, R., and S. Shapiro. "Sex Differences in Personality Traits of Female and Male Master of Business Administration Students." *Journal of Applied Psychology* 67 (June 1982): 306-10.

Stephens, G. E., and A. S. DeNisi. "Women As Managers: Attitudes and Attributions for Performance by Men and Women." *Academy of Management Journal* 23 (June 1980): 355-61.

Strober, M. "The MBA: Same Passport to Success for Women and Men?" In P. A. Wallace, ed., *Women in the Workplace*, ch. 2, pp. 25-44. Boston, Mass.: Auburn House Publishing Co., 1982.

"Survey Finds Women MBAs Still Trail." *The Boston Globe*, June 23, 1983.

"Survey of Women Executives." In *The Wall Street Journal*. New York: Dow Jones and Company Inc., October 1984.

Sutton, C. D., and K. K. Moore. "Executive Women—Twenty Years Later." *Harvard Business Review* 63 (September-October 1985): 42-66.

Tangri, S. S. *Effects of Background, Personality, College and Post-College Experience on Women's Post-Graduate Employment: Final Report*. Washington, D.C.: U.S. Department of Labor, Manpower Administration, 1974.

Taylor, A., III. "Why Women Managers Are Bailing Out." *Fortune* 114 (August 18, 1986): 16-23.

Terborg, J. R. "Women in Management: A Research Review." *Journal of Applied Psychology* 62 (1977): 647-64.

Terborg, J. R.; L. H. Peters; D. Ilgen; and F. Smith. "Organizational and Personal Correlates of Attitudes Toward Women as Managers." *Academy of Management Journal* 20 (1977): 89-100.

Trieman, D. J., and K. Terreck. "Sex and the Process of Status Attainment: A Comparison of Working Women and Men." *American Sociological Review* 40 (April 1975): 174-200.

Trieman, D. J., and P. A. Roos. "Sex and Earnings in Industrial Society: A Nine Nation Comparison." *American Journal of Sociology* 89 (November 1983): 612-50.

Tsui, A. S., and B. A. Gutek. "A Role Set Analysis of Gender Differences in Performances, Affective Relationships, and Career Success of Industrial Middle Managers." *Academy of Management Journal* 27 (September 1984): 619-35.

Tucker, S. "Careers of Men and Women MBAs." *Work and Occupations* 12 (May 1985): 166-85.

U.S. Department of Labor, Women's Bureau. *Women in Management*. Washington, D.C.: U.S. Government Printing Office, 1980.

U.S. Equal Employment Opportunity Commission (EEOC). "Job Patterns for Minorities and Women in Private Industry." Washington, D.C.: U.S. Government Printing Office, various years.

Waite, L. J., and R. M. Stolzenberg. "Intended Childbearing and Labor Force Participation of Young Women: Insights From Nonrecursive Models." *American Sociological Review* 41 (April 1976): 235-52.

Wallace, P. A. *Equal Employment Opportunity and the AT&T Case.* Cambridge, Mass.: MIT Press, 1976.

Wallace, P. A., ed. *Women in the Workplace.* Boston, Mass.: Auburn House Publishing Co., 1982.

Wertheim, E. G.; C. Spatz Windom; and L. H. Wortzel. "Multivariate Analysis of Male and Female Professional Career Choice Correlates." *Journal of Applied Psychology* 63 (1978): 234-42.

"When a Daughter Takes Over the Family Business." *Business Week* (March 29, 1982): 172-75.

"Why so Few Women Have Made it to the Top." *Business Week* (June 5, 1978): 99-102.

Wolf, W. C., and N. D. Fligstein. "Sexual Stratification: Differences in Power in the Work Setting." Institute for Research on Poverty Discussion Papers, University of Wisconsin at Madison, 1978.

"Women at the B-School Today." *Fortune* 108 (July 11, 1983): 72.

"Women at Work." *Business Week* (January 28, 1985): 80-85.

"Women Finally Get Mentors of Their Own." *Business Week* (October 23, 1978): 74-80.

The Woodlands Group. "Management Development Roles: Coach, Sponsor and Mentor." *Personnel Journal* 59 (November 1980): 918-21.

Wortman, M. S., Jr. "An Overview of the Research on Women in Management: A Typology and Prospectus." In H. J. Bernardin, ed., *Women in the Work-Force*, ch. 1, pp. 1-28. New York: Praeger Publishers, 1982.

"You've Come a Long Way Baby—But Not as Far as You Thought." *Business Week* (October 1, 1984): 126-31.

Zappert, L. T., and H. M. Weinstein. "Sex Differences in the Impact of Work on Physical and Psychological Health." *American Journal of Psychiatry* 142 (October 1985): 1174-78.

Zey, M. G. *The Mentor Connection.* Homewood, Ill.: Dow Jones-Irvin, 1984.

BLACK MANAGERS

America, R. F., and B. E. Anderson. *Moving Ahead: Black Managers in American Business.* New York: McGraw-Hill Book Co., 1978.

Alderfer, C. P.; C. J. Alderfer; L. Tucker; and R. Tucker. "Diagnosing Race Relations in Management." *Journal of Applied Behavioral Science* 16 (June 1980): 135-66.

Bay, J. C. "Determinants of the Upward Mobility of Asian Americans in General Management." Master's thesis, Sloan School of Management, Massachusetts Institute of Technology, 1987.

Bell, E. L. "The Power Within: Bicultural Life Structures and Stress Among Black Women." Ph.D. dissertation Case Western Reserve, 1986 (unpublished).

Brown, H. "A Study of Career Patterns and Graduate Educational Experiences of a Selected Group of Minority MBAs Who Graduated Between January 1969 and January 1974." Ph.D. dissertation, University of Wisconsin at Madison, 1975. (Unpublished.)

Brown, H. A., and D. L. Ford, Jr. "An Exploratory Analysis of Discrimination in the Employment of Black MBA Graduates." *Journal of Applied Psychology* 62 (February 1977): 50-56.

Brown, H. A., and D. L. Ford, Jr. "Employment Progress and Job Satisfaction of Minority MBA Graduates." Paper No. 502. Indianapolis, Ind.: Krannert Graduate School of Industrial Administration, Purdue University, 1975.

"Progress Report on the Black Executive: The Top Spots Are Still Elusive." *Business Week* (February 20, 1984): 104.

Campbell, B. M. "Black Executives and Corporate Stress." *The New York Times Magazine* (December 12, 1982): 36-39, 100-7.

Clarke, R., ed. "The Black MBA: Needed: Unlimited Access." *Contact* 5 (Winter 1973): 7-37.

Council for Opportunity in Graduate Management Education (COGME). "Recent Minority Graduates of the COGME Member Schools." 1978. (Unpublished.)

Cox, T., Jr., and S. Nkomo. "Differential Performance Appraisal Criteria: A Field Study of Black and White Managers." *Group and Organization Studies* 11 (1986): 101-19.

Davis, G., and C. Watson. *Black Life in Corporate America*. Garden City, N.Y.: Doubleday and Co., 1982.

Davis, G., and C. Watson. "The Black Gamesman." *Psychology Today* 16 (August 1982): 56-64.

Dentzer, S., and R. Michael. "They Shall Overcome." *Newsweek* 101 (May 23, 1983): 60-62.

Dickens, F., Jr., and J. B. Dickens. *The Black Manager*. New York: AMACOM, 1982.

The Executive Study Conference. "On-the-Job Experience of Negro Managers." Princeton, N.J.: Educational Testing Service, 1964.

The Executive Study Conference. "Selecting and Training Negroes for Managerial Positions." Princeton, N.J.: Educational Testing Service, 1964.

Fernandez, J. P. *Racism and Sexism in Corporate Life*. Lexington, Mass.: Lexington Books, 1981.

Fernandez, J. P. *Black Managers in White Corporations*. New York: John Wiley and Sons, 1975.

Fields, C. L., and E. S. Freeman. "Black Professionals: The Gap is Not Closing." *MBA* 6 (January 1972): 73-84.

Ford, D. L., Jr. "Perspective: Minorities in Organizations." Paper No. 501. Krannert Graduate School of Industrial Administration, Purdue University, 1975.

Ford, D. L., Jr. "Job-Related Stress of the Minority Professional: An Exploratory Analysis and Suggestions for Future Research." In T. A. Beehr and R. S. Bhagat, eds., *Human Stress and Cognition in Organizations: An Integrative Perspective*, ch. 11, pp. 287-324. New York: John Wiley and Sons, 1973.

Freeman, R. *Black Elites: The New Market for Highly Educated Black America.* New York: McGraw-Hill Book Co., 1976.

Fulbright, K. L. "The Myth of the Double-Advantage: Black Women in Management." Ph.D. dissertation, Sloan School of Management, Massachusetts Institute of Technology, 1985.

Gains, S. "Black Interest in MBAs Waning." *Chicago Tribune*, March 1, 1987.

Greenberger, R. S. "Up the Ladder: Many Black Managers Hope to Enter Ranks of Top Management." *The Wall Street Journal*, January 15, 1981.

Heckman, J. J., and B. Payner. "Determining the Impact of Federal Antidiscrimination Policy on the Economic Status of Blacks." July 1988. (Unpublished.)

Heidrick and Struggles, Inc. *Profile of Black Executives.* Chicago: Heidrick and Struggles, 1979.

Hicks, J. P. "A Black's Climb To Executive Suite." *The New York Times*, May 22, 1987.

Hicks, J P. "Black Professionals Refreshen Their Careers." *The New York Times*, November 29, 1985.

Hills, G. E. "The Graduate Schools and Minority Integration: The Black MBA." *American Assembly of Collegiate Schools of Business Bulletin* (April 1973): 28-43.

Holsendolph, R. "Black Executives in a Nearly All White World." *Fortune* 87 (September 1972): 140-51.

Hymowitz, C. "Many Blacks Jump Off the Corporate Ladder to be Entrepreneurs." *The Wall Street Journal*, August 2, 1984.

Irons, S., and G. Moore. *Black Managers: The Case of the Banking Industry.* New York: Praeger Publishers, 1985.

Jones, E. W., Jr. "Black Managers: The Dream Deferred." *Harvard Business Review* 64 (May/June 1986): 84-93.

Jones, E. W., Jr. "What It's Like to be a Black Manager." *Harvard Business Review* 51 (July/August 1973): 108-16.

Kaufman, J. "Black Executives Say Prejudice Still Impedes Their Path to the Top." *The Wall Street Journal*, July 9, 1980.

Lee, E. D. "Is the MBA Still a Golden Passport?" *Black Enterprise* 11 (February 1981): 43-46.

Leinster, C. "Black Executives: How They Are Doing." *Fortune* (January 1988): 109-20.

Leonard, J. "Anti-Discrimination or Reverse Discrimination: The Impact of Changing Demographics, Title VII, and Affirmative Action on Productivity." *The Journal of Human Resources* (Spring 1984): 145-73.

McCall, N. "Does MBA Stand for Making it Big in America?" *Black Enterprise* 16 (October 1985): 87–90.

Recruiting Management Consultants. *A Study of Black Male Professionals in Industry.* Springfield, Va.: National Technical Information Service, 1973.

Smithers, Lester, Jr., and A. Beaty, Jr. "Comparative Analysis of Career Anchors of Black Professionals and Managers in the Private and Public Sector." Master's thesis, Sloan School of Management, Massachusetts Institute of Technology, 1985.

Taylor, S. "The Black Executive and the Corporation: A Difficult Fit." *MBA* 6 (January 1972): 8.

Taylor, S. A. "Action Oriented Research: An Application of Organizational Behavior Methodology to Black American Executives in Major Corporations." Proceedings of the Thirty-Second Annual Meeting of the Academy of Management, Minneapolis, Minnesota, 1972.

Thomas, D. A. "Black Experiences of Gaining Mentoring and Sponsorship in Organizations." Paper for the Annual Meeting of the Academy of Management. New Orleans, Louisiana, June 1987.

Thomas, D. A., and C. P. Alderfer. "The Influence of Race on Career Dynamics: Theory and Research on Minority Career Experiences." To appear in M. Arthur; D. Hall; and B. Lawrence, eds., *Handbook of Career Theory.* New York: Cambridge University Press, forthcoming.

U. S. Department of Labor. "A Study of Black Male Professionals in Industry." Manpower Research No. 26, Washington, D.C.: U. S. Government Printing Office, 1973.

U. S. Equal Employment Opportunity Commission (EEOC). *Job Patterns of Minorities and Women in Private Industry.* Washington, D.C.: U. S. Government Printing Office, various years.

Wallace, P. A. "The Private Sector and Equal Employment Opportunity in the 1980's." *Rutgers Law Review* 37 (1985): 1041–53.

Watson, J. G., and S. Barone. "The Self Concept, Personal Values, and Motivational Orientations of Black and White Managers." *Academy of Management Journal* 19 (March 1976): 36–48.

Watson, J., and J. Williams. "Relationship Between Managerial Values and Managerial Success of Black and White Managers." *Journal of Applied Psychology* 62 (1977): 203–207.

Williams, L. I., IV. "On Recruitment of Blacks at the Sloan School of Management." Master's thesis, Sloan School of Management, Massachusetts Institute of Technology, 1976.

INDEX

ABOUT THE AUTHOR

Phyllis A. Wallace, Ph.D., is Professor of Management, *Emerita* at the Sloan School of Management at the Massachusetts Institute of Technology. She has been actively engaged as a researcher, teacher, and consultant on issues of human resource management. Her publications include: *Pathway to Work: Unemployment Among Black Teenage Females* (1974); *Equal Employment Opportunity and the AT&T Case* (1976); *Women, Minorities and Employment Discrimination*, with Annette LaMond (1977); *Black Women in the Labor Force* (1980); and *Women in the Workplace*, editor (1982). Professor Wallace has viewed many of the issues raised in this book from her perspective as a director of several corporate boards. During 1988 she has served as the National President of the Industrial Relations Research Association (IRRA). She recently received a Distinguished Service Award from the Harvard Business School.